BAY CITY GREY: select Bay City, Michigan buildings in ink drawings

This book is not a historical book of Bay City, Michigan buildings but there are examples of historical buildings inside but there are also "new" buildings that wouldn't be deemed as "historical". All the buildings in the city of Bay City are NOT illustrated in this book either. There are select buildings that were chosen by me.

The images in this book were done on watercolor paper with Black India ink done with several brushes and a dip pen. This is not a how to book but rather it showcases images chosen by me to illustrate what a culturally rich area Bay City , Michigan is. See figure one that illustrates what these tools look like.

I was not born and raised in Bay City, Michigan. I came to this city on the coat tails of my ex-wife. My son, Cameron, currently lives here. Instead of traveling to exotic   places faraway , I found interesting local sights to do drawings from. I chose to stick to "home" and I am glad I did !

There are some interesting things to draw right here in Bay City , Michigan!!!!! From the historical buildings such as the Trombley house and the many churches such as St. Stanislaus Kostka Church, to the more unique buildings such as Delta Planetarium and local restaurants such as Rudy's Red Lion Diner and Stock Pot Diner.

I hope you like my ink drawings that showcase this "hidden gem" in the state of Michigan : Bay City !! All the images are of India ink drawings on watercolor paper with the exception of the few examples in the appendix I chose to redo some of images with acrylic paint in color.

I CHOSE TO DO ALMOST ALL THE IMAGES IN BLACK AND WHITE TO GIVE IT THE FEEL OF A HISTORICAL BOOK WITH ARCHIVAL IMAGES. I AM VERY FOND OF BLACK AND WHITE PHOTOGRAPHS SINCE THESE GIVE THE IMPRESSION OF AN INK DRAWING .

I HOPE YOU ENJOY MY "HISTORICAL" IMAGES ,

Thanks,
        Patrick B. Humphreys
        Bay City, Michigan

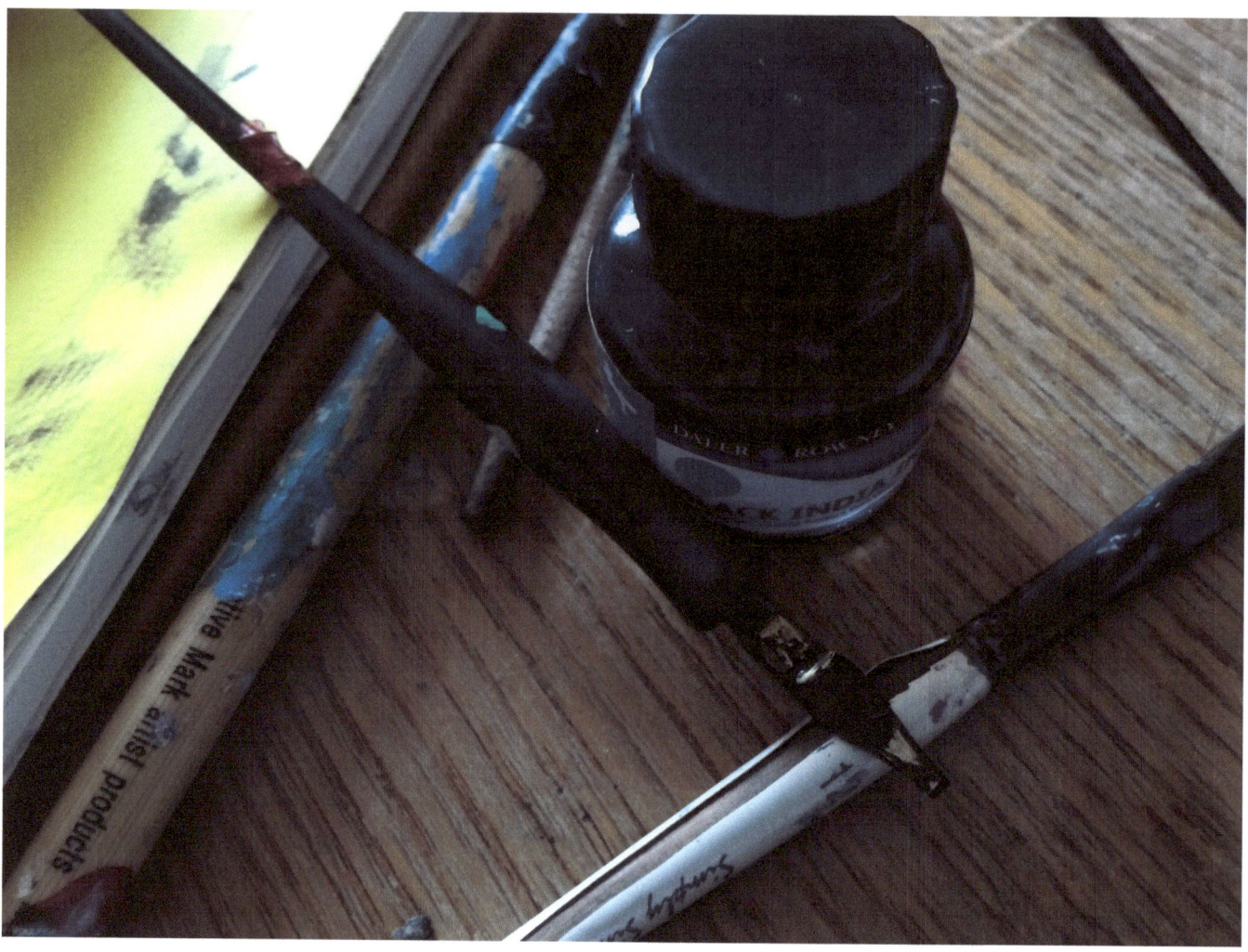

Figure 1- above. This image shows the tools I used to create 97% of the drawings in this book. It shows an India ink bottle, several brushes , and a dip pen. A rather dirty dip pen !!! At the right side of the photograph you get a glance at the last necessary item : the watercolor paper. With these minimal tools most of the drawings were created in this book. The last images in the appendix shows several of the buildings in this book in COLOR. I used acrylic paint in addition to the India ink. I PERSONALLY FEEL THE BLACK AND WHITE IMAGES WORK BETTER THAN THE COLOR ONES !!!

THE PLATES

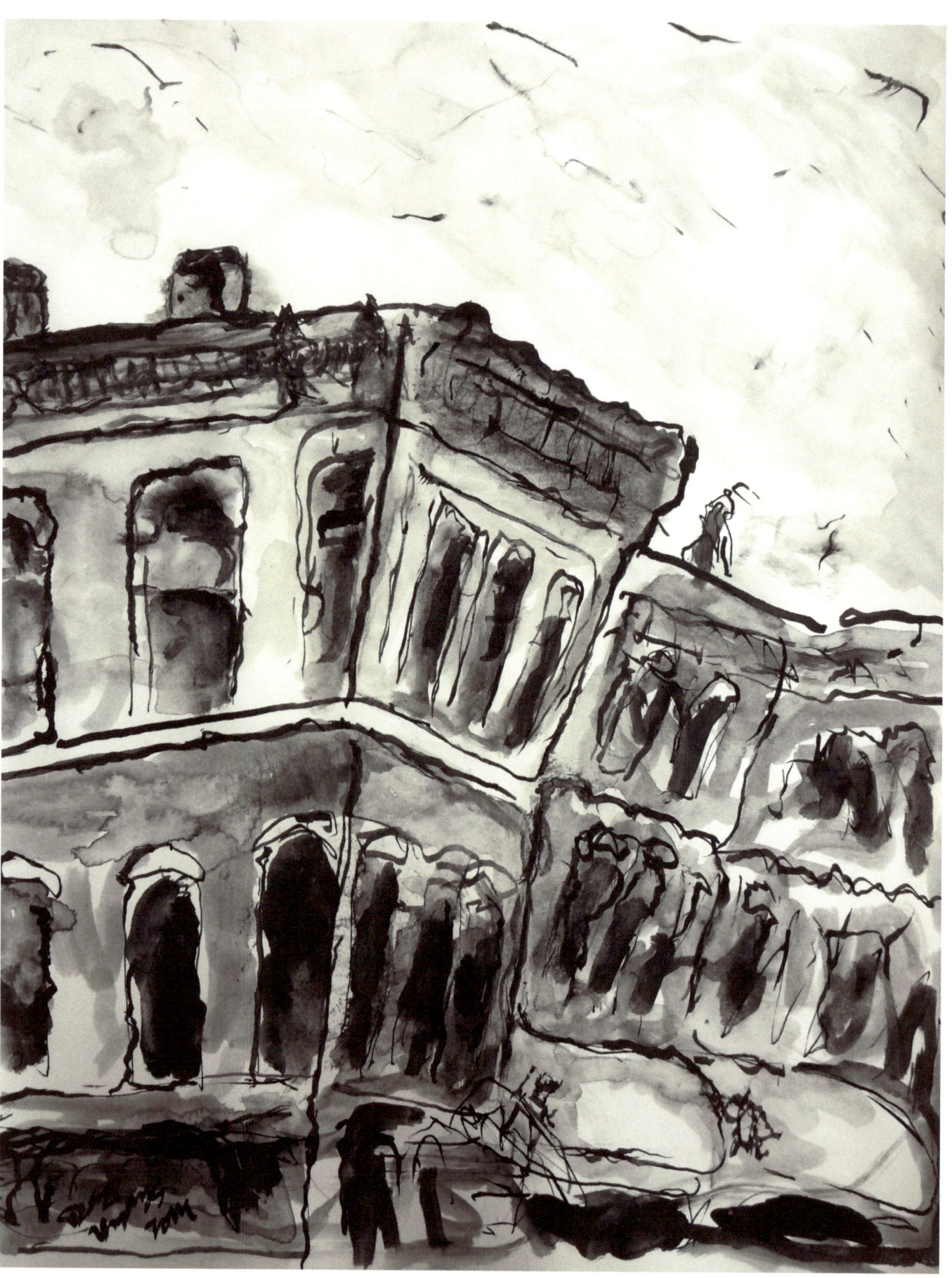

Figure 2: PREVIOUS PAGE :this image started it all. This building is not identified. While down at the C.A.T. WORK Art Gallery in Bay City , I noticed a book on the table. The book was "Bay City : Then and Now " by Leon Kartzinger , ISBN : 9780738533315, Arcadia Publishing, 2004. On the cover of the book was a photograph of a building in Bay City. I brought with me , India ink, brushes, dip pen and some watercolor paper to the gallery to do artwork with. The owner of the gallery , Tom Larson , lets me paint in the backroom of the gallery. THANKS TOM !! THIS IMAGE IS THE ONLY IMAGE I CREATED FROM SOMEONELSE'S PHOTOGRAPH . THE REST OF THE IMAGES WERE DONE FROM PERSONAL PHOTOGRAPHS TAKEN AROUND BAY CITY, MICHIGAN.

Figure 3: NEXT PAGE : This image is of the Sage Library located at 100 East Midland Avenue in the city of Bay City. This structure was constructed in 1884 for the sole purpose of being a library branch of the Bay County Library System. IT IS STILL IN USE AFTER 130 YEARS !!! Still a beautiful building !!! This drawing does not show much of the building. Friends have told me that there is not enough of the building portrayed to identify the building. Maybe, maybe not !! Even if you can't identify the building it is a "good" drawing.

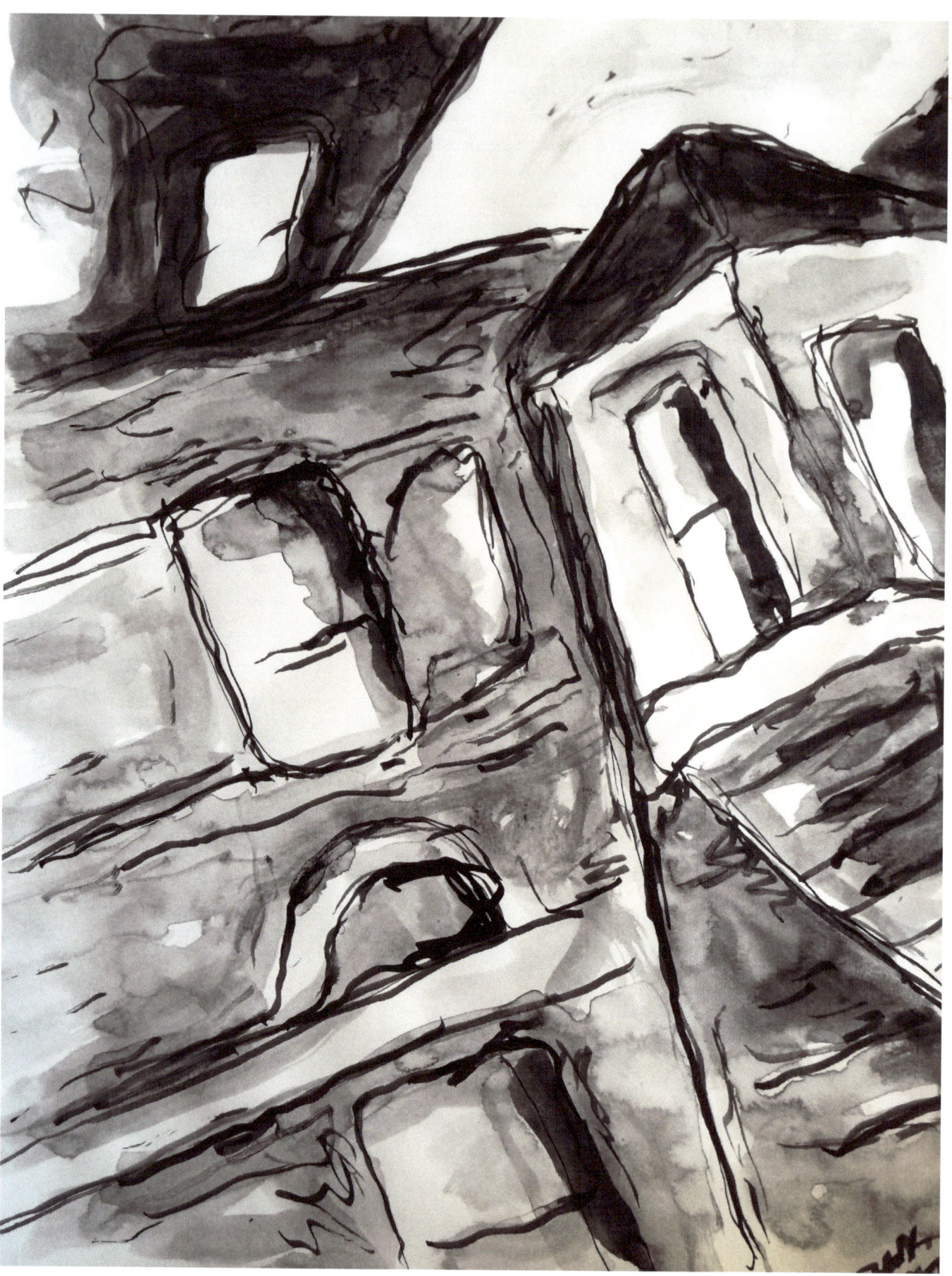

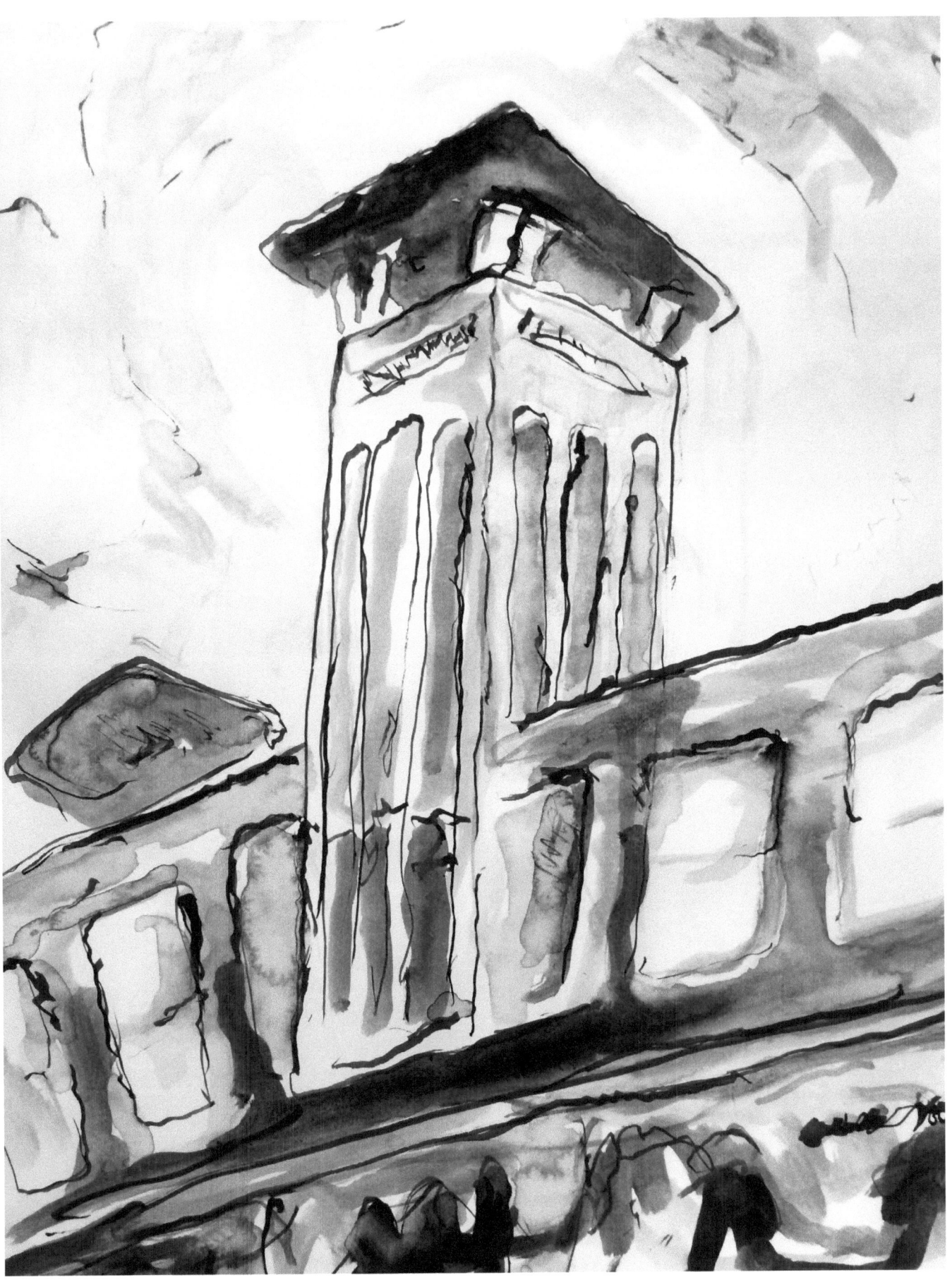

Figure 4: PREVIOUS PAGE – this image is of Pere Marquette-Union Passenger Station at 919 Boutell Place. This building was originally used as a train station built in 1904. It's purpose is very different today. It is used as a place to attend after a wedding or baby shower. A very different kind of passage then one by a train. A beginning of a marriage er a birth of a life !!! I hope my drawings provide as much thought as that. So step "aboard" this "train". Don't let it "run" over your feelings. Don't "miss" the thought train. Let it be "deep" inside . CATCH THE TRAIN .

Figure 5 : NEXT PAGE- this image is another view of the historical Sage Library but more of the building is shown. The iconic female sculpture in an exterior nave makes this building easily recognizable to locals. All of the readers of this book perhaps won't recognize the building but it still is a successful drawing.

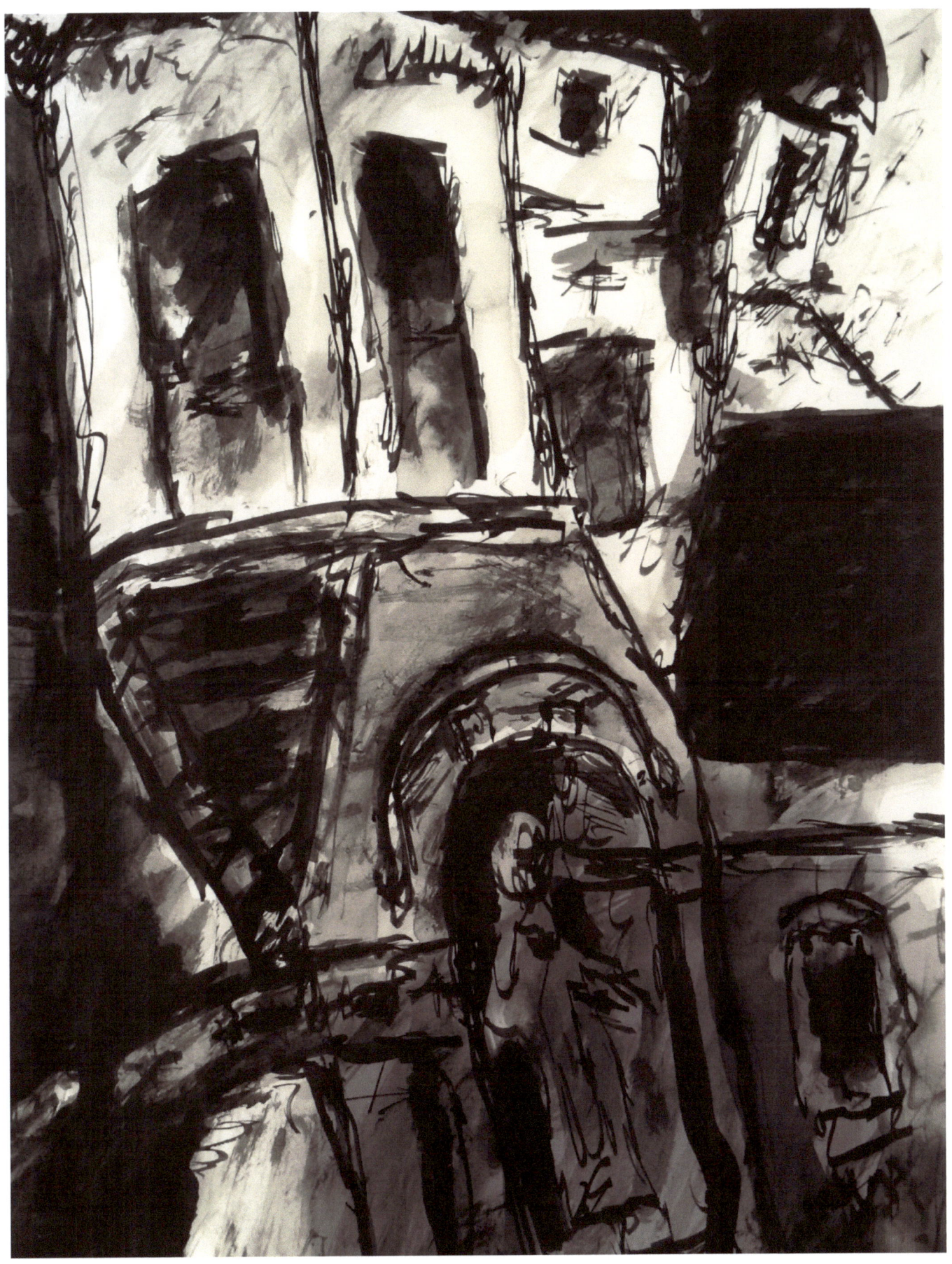

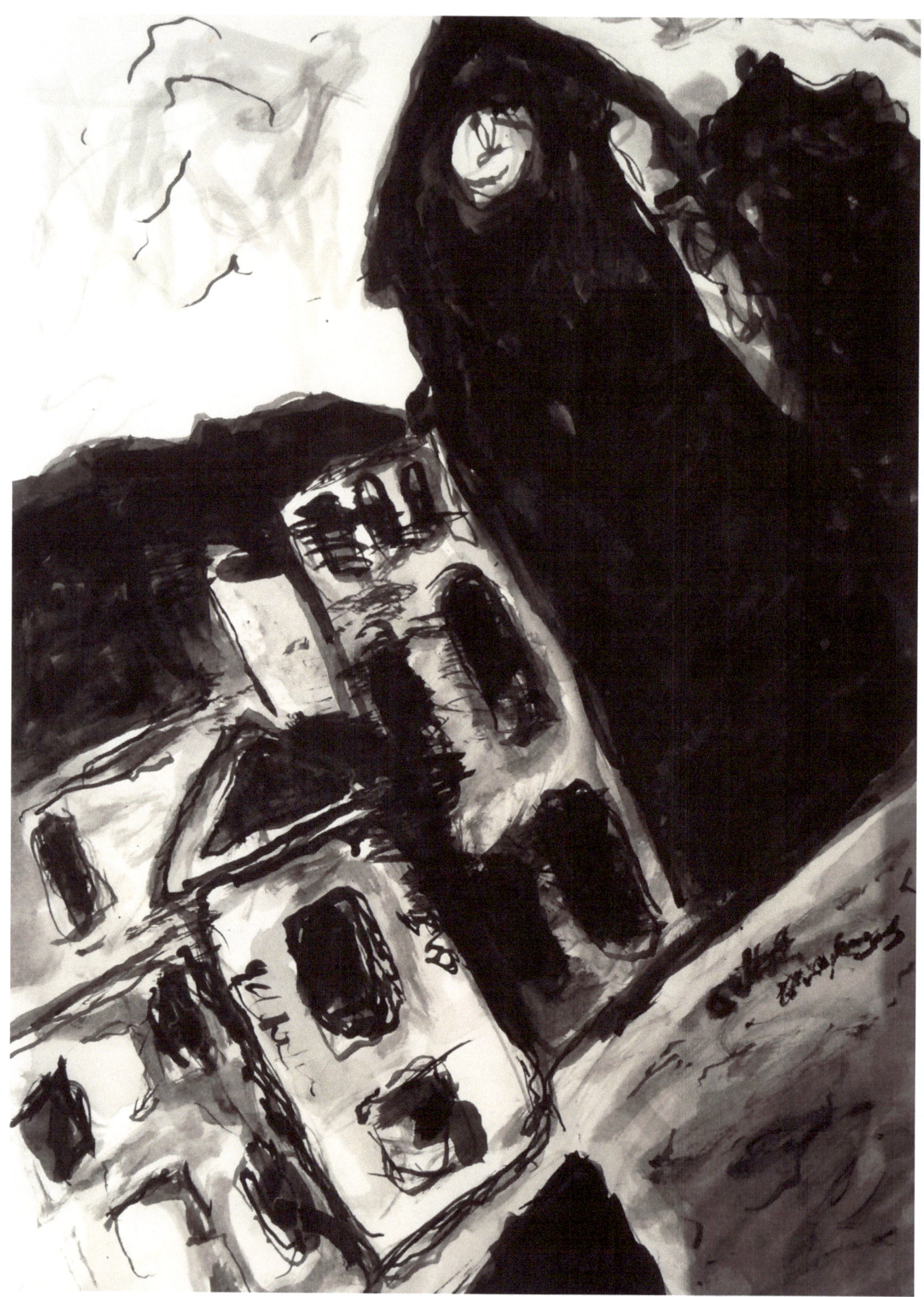

Figure 6-PREVOIUS PAGE- this image is of City Hall. This building recently was renovated. It took 3 years to finish !!!! Longer than it was to build the Mackinac Bridge !! On a brighter note my drawing did NOT take three years to complete !!! Much less than that !! This image is based upon my personal photograph. I was looking up at the building . It created a very strange view that abstracted the image. I personally like the "weird" angle. HOW ABOUT YOU ??

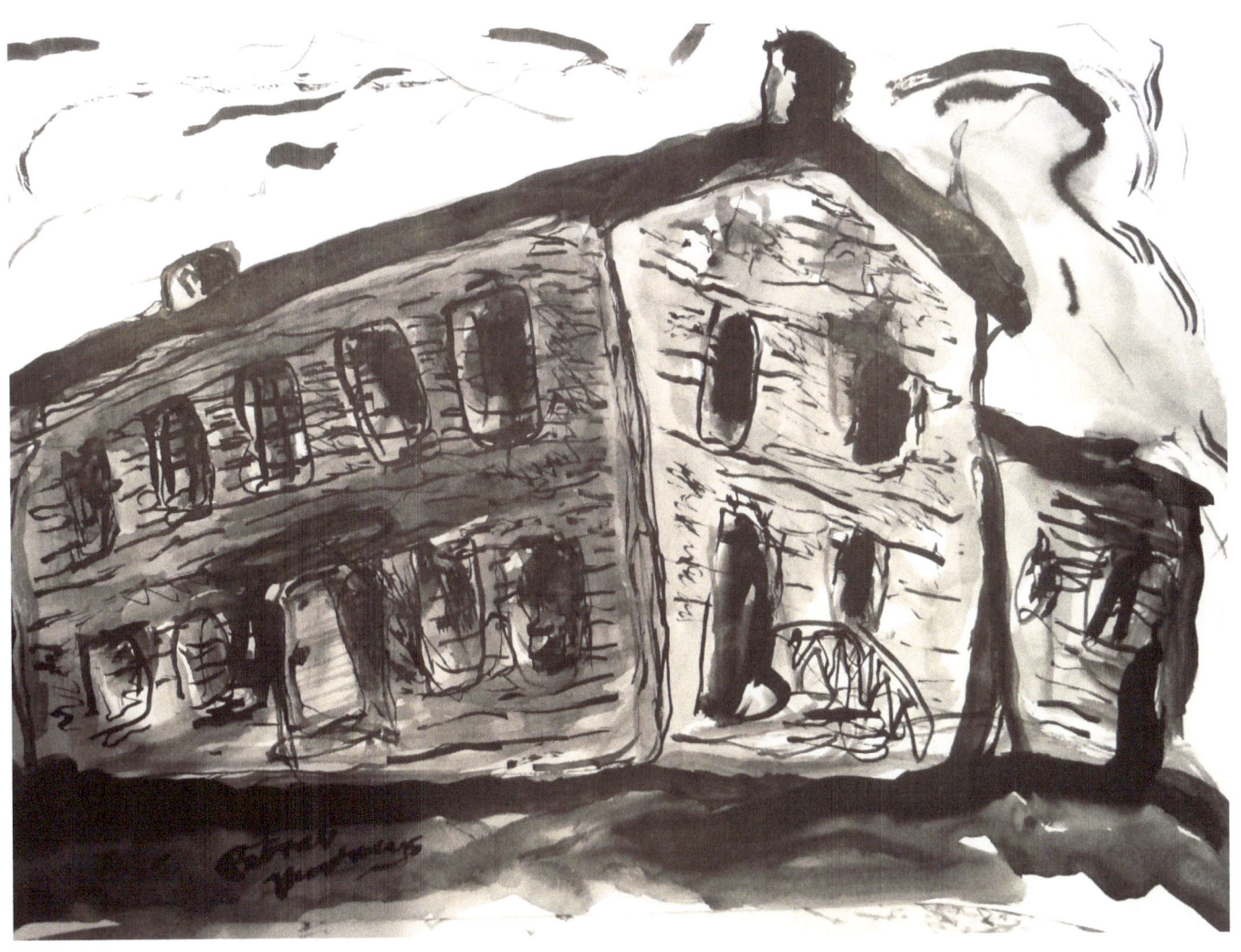

FIGURE 7 -ABOVE- this drawing is of the Trombley House. The oldest building in Bay City. It was built in 1836 and moved to Veterans Memorial Park. This building is the center of the annual "River Of Time" festival. This festival is the reenactment of life in the 1800's. Very interesting !!! If you are here during the summer I highly recommend it ! I also recommend this drawing !

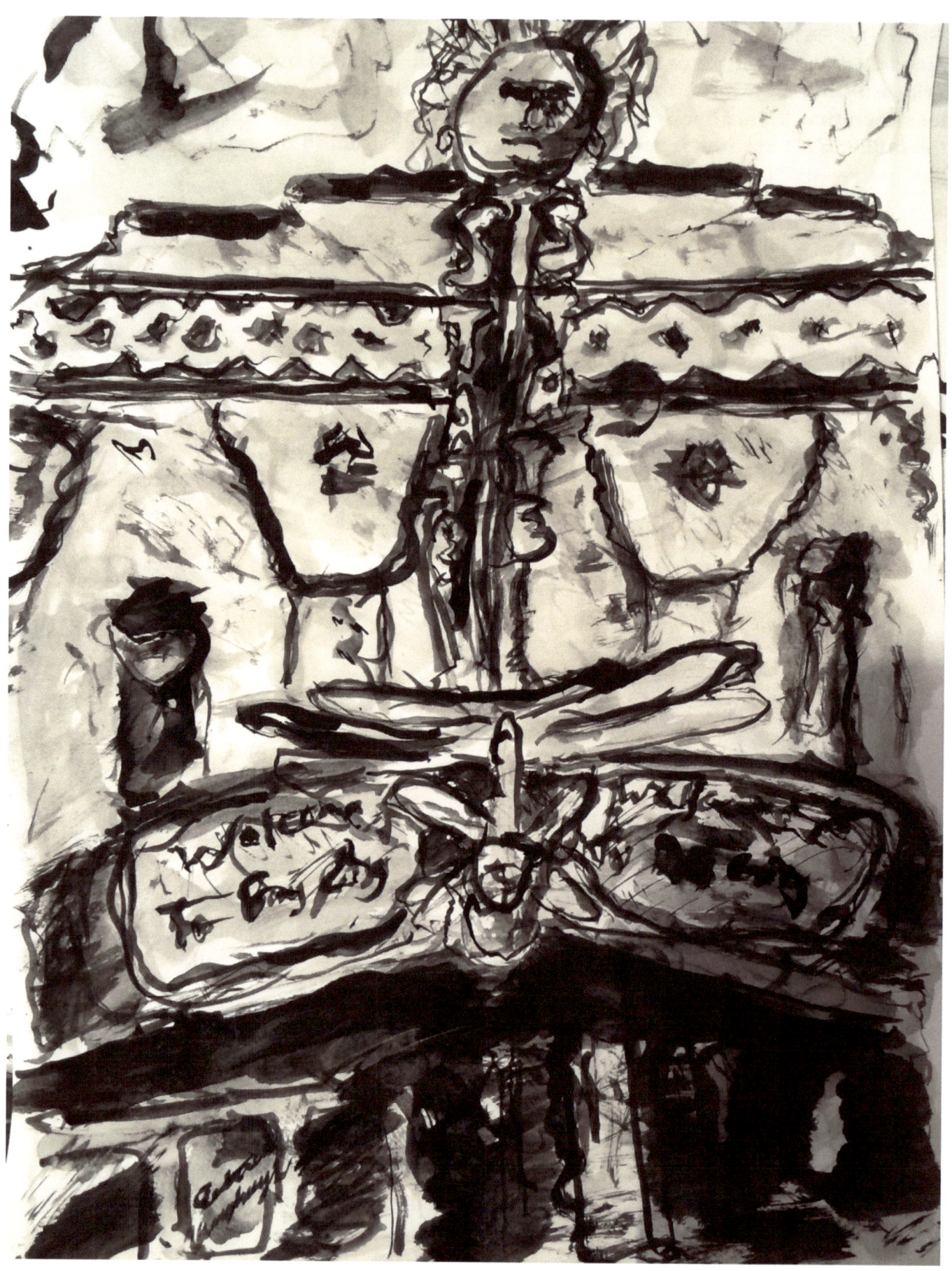

Figure 8-PREVIOUS PAGE- this drawing is of the State Theater. This building is very interesting. The outside as well as the inside features a Mayan theme. Notice the Mayan head on the top and another smaller one near the bottom of the drawing. I saw a movie with my son, Cameron, here . Very interesting !!!! Historical and beautiful inside and out !!

Figure 9-NEXT PAGE -another view of the State Theater. This time more of the building is shown not just the distinctive Mayan head. Actually in this drawing I chose not to include the Mayan head at all but rather drew the word : STATE and included the sign in the image. The sign that show what is playing at the theater is not readable. That was my intention. To give the impression of the distinctive building and not focus on the words in the sign. The sign : STATE clearly identifies this as the State Theater. This is a definite "stop" in Bay City !!! I just hope you "stop" for a moment to look at my drawing !

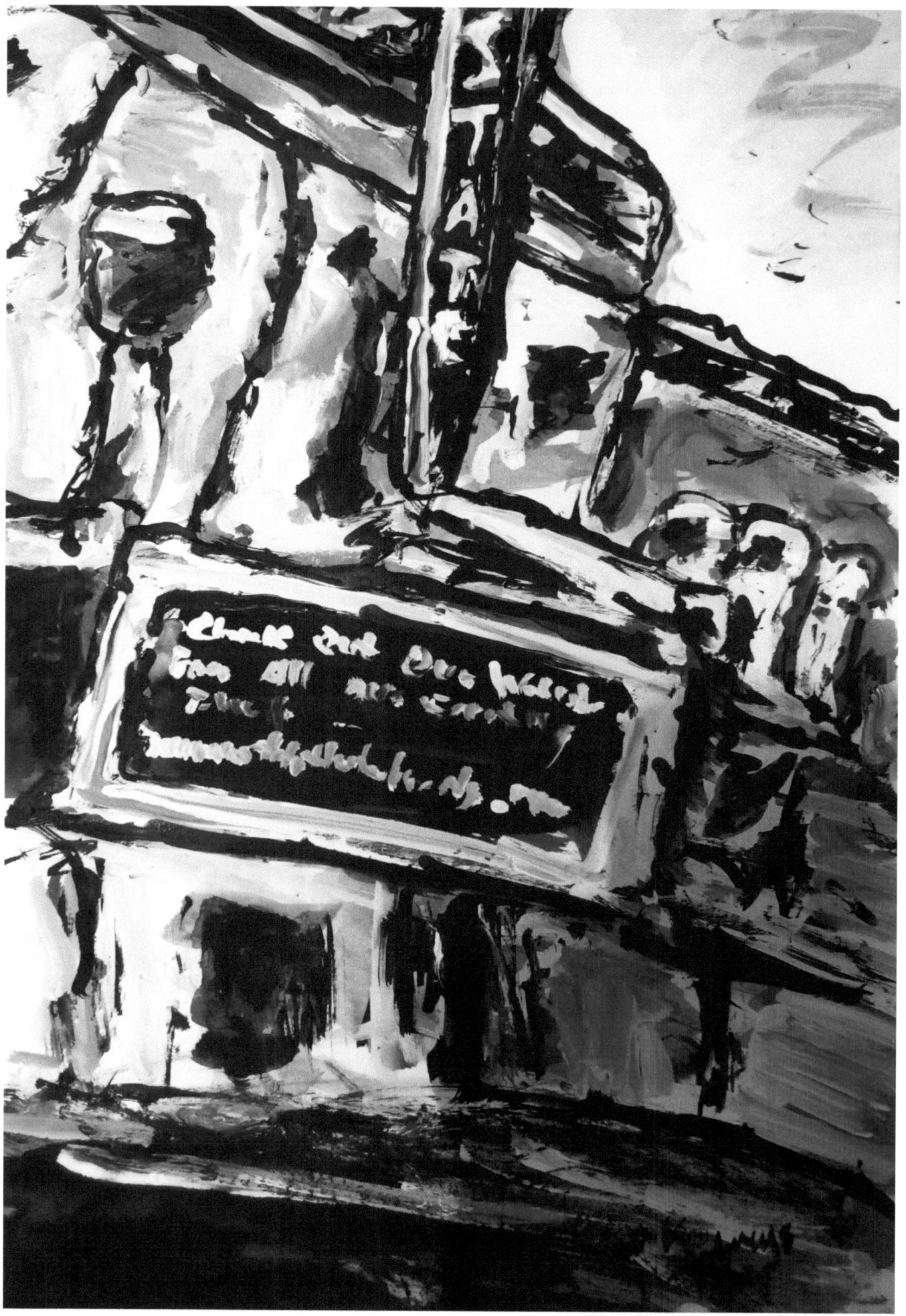

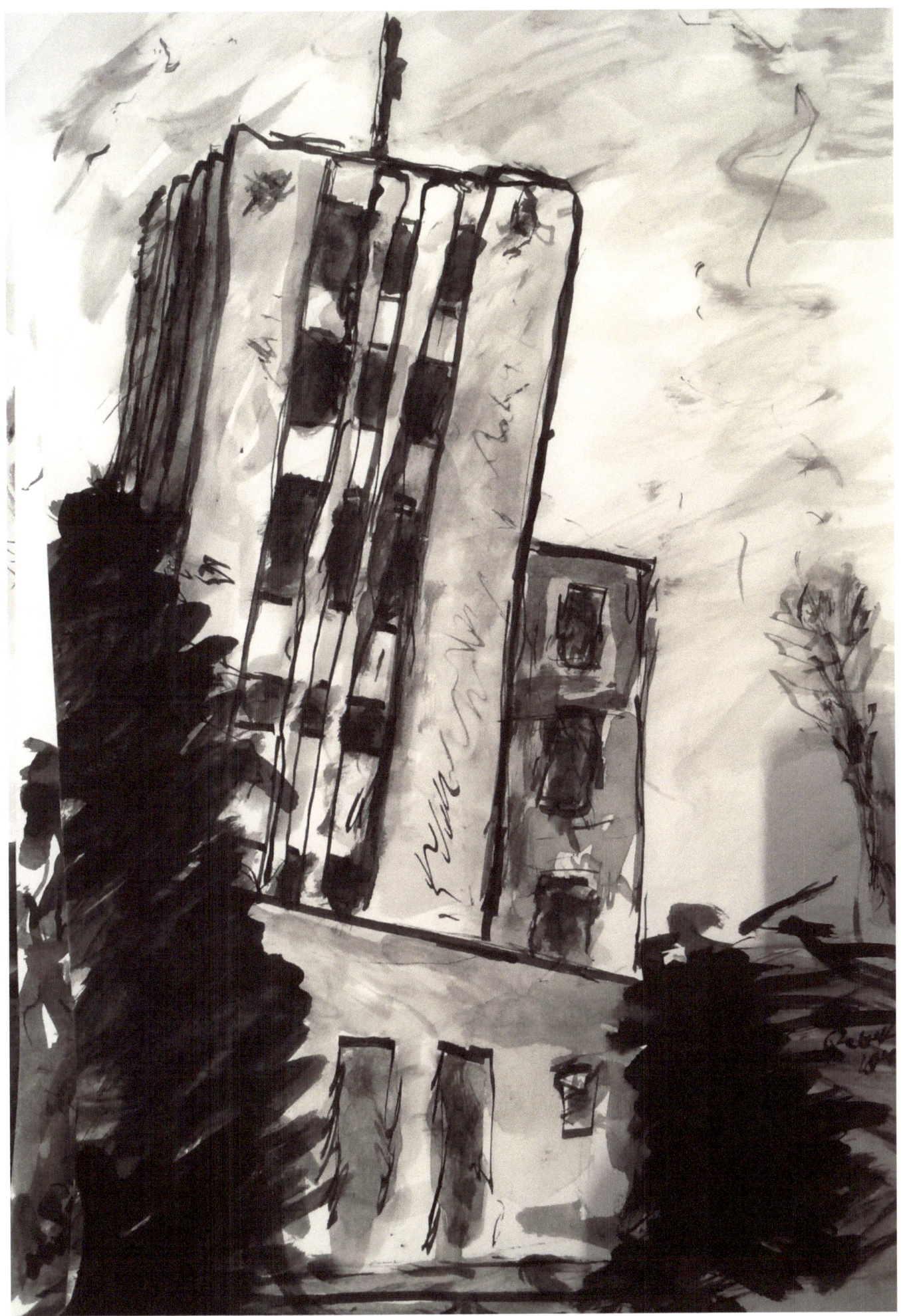

Figure 10- PREVIOUS PAGE- this image is of the Bay County building. It was built in 1933 at 515 Center Avenue in Bay City. It is still used for Bay City government. There is a courthouse inside among many other government offices. Luckily I have never had to go inside this building for any legal problems !!! But don't let that stop you from admiring this spectacular building !! This is one of my favorite drawings of Bay City buildings !! Do you think so ??

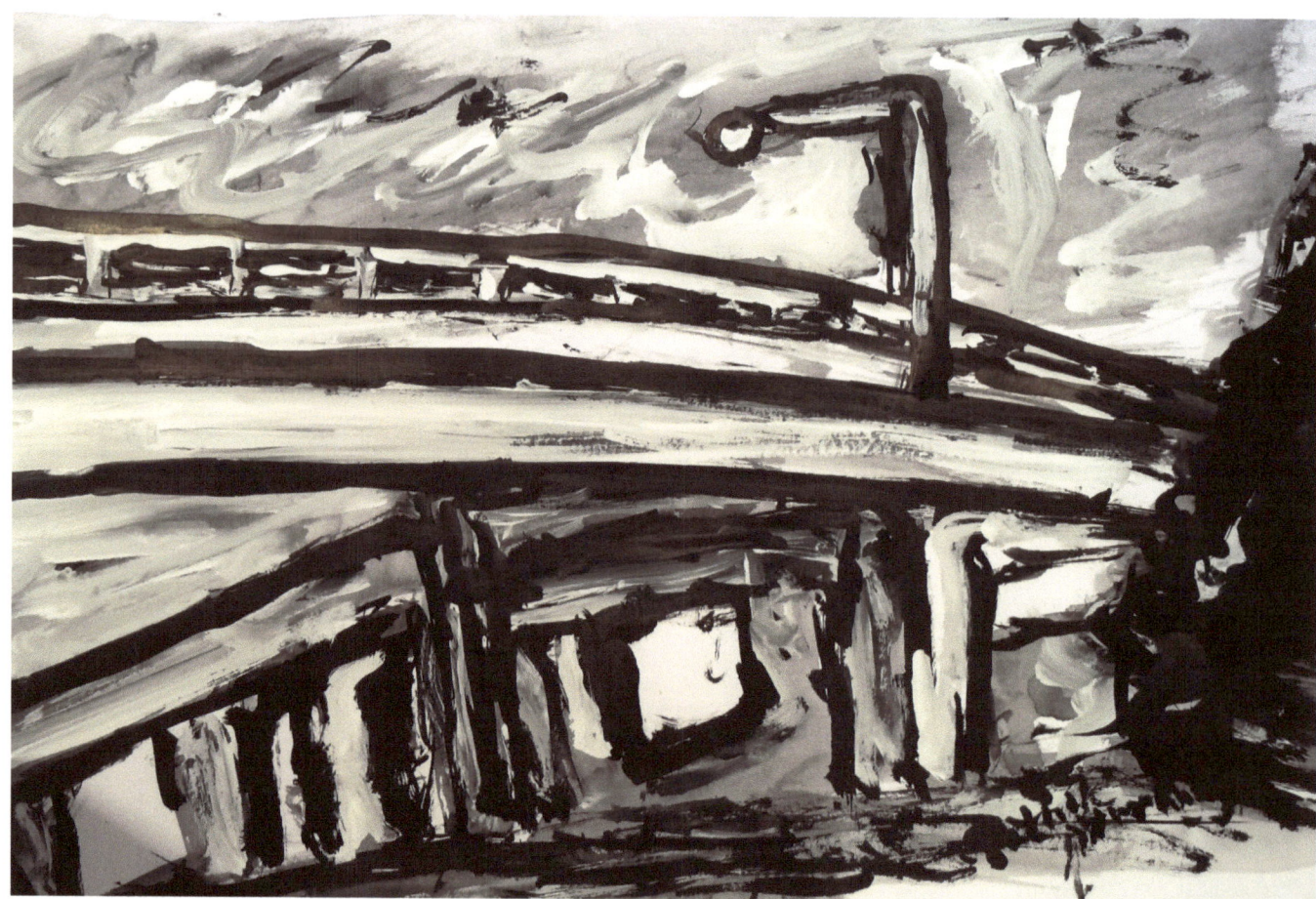

Figure 11-ABOVE -this is NOT TECHNICALLY A BUILDING !! BUT IT IS OF A THING OF MUCH IMPORTANCE TO BAY CITY .IT IS OF A BRIDGE. There are four drawbridges in Bay City : Liberty Bridge, Veterans Memorial Bridge, Independence Bridge and Lafayette Avenue Bridge. I based this drawing on a personal photograph taken while driving under the Veterans Memorial Bridge. There is just enough detail to make it recognizable as a bridge .

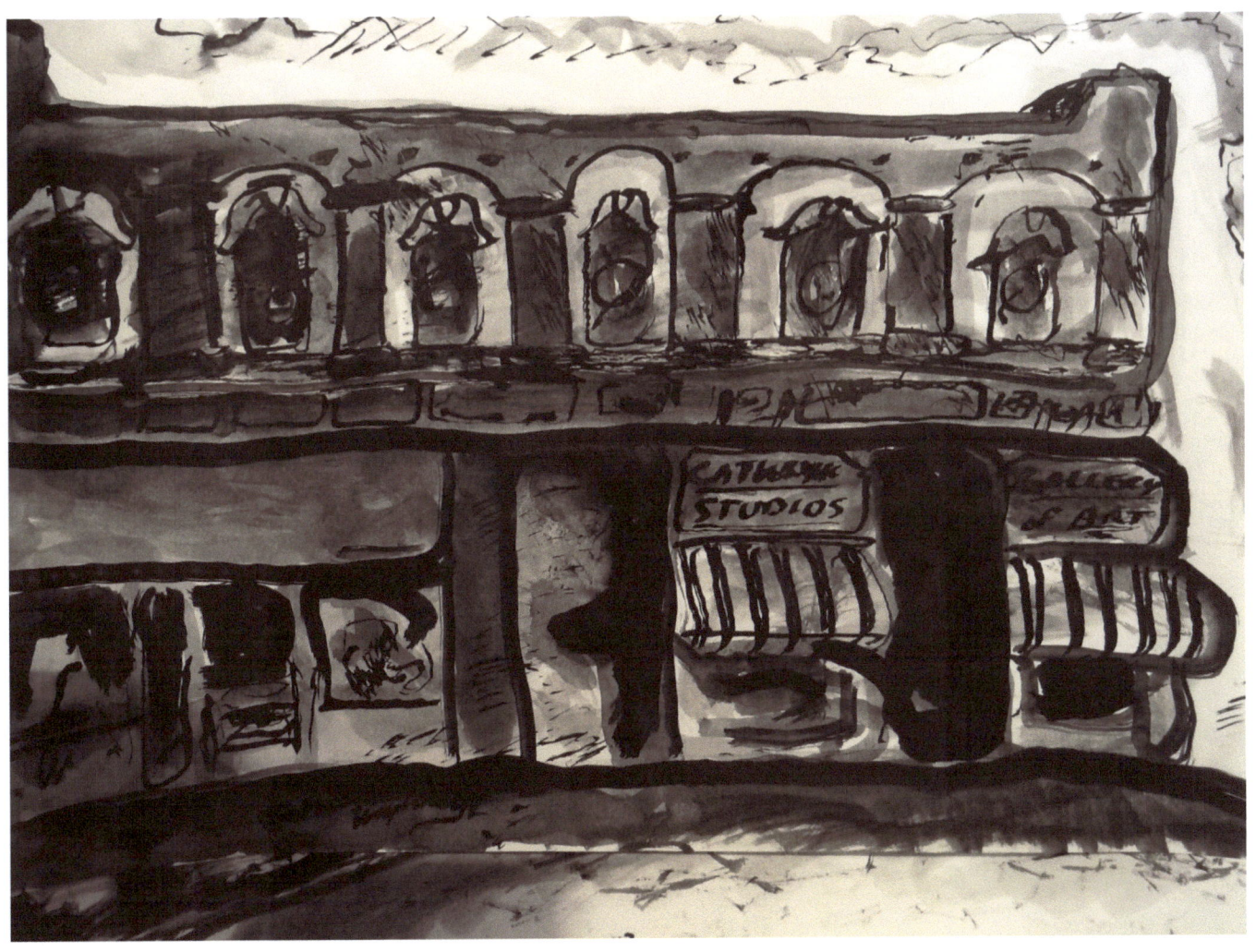

Figure 12-ABOVE- although this building is not listed on the registrar of historical buildings in Bay City it is VERY IMPORTANT TO ME. IT IS WHERE I DISPLAY MUCH OF MY WORK AND WITHIN ITS WALLS I HAVE CREATED AT LEAST HALF OF THE WORKS IN THIS BOOK. THE OWNER TOM LARSON IS A GREAT ADVOCATE FOR ART IN BAY CITY!! NOT ONLY IS HE A NICE GUY , LETS ME DISPLAY MY WORK BUT HE IS A GREAT ARTIST AS WELL . I CAN'T THANK HIM ENOUGH !!!! THANKS !!!!!!

Figure 13-NEXT PAGE -this is another drawing based upon the building that houses the C.A.T. WORK Art Gallery at 514 Washington Avenue, Bay City, MI 48708, (989) 893-2771, Ext. 6. If you ever get a chance to visit Bay City, this place should be number 1 on your list !! THE ART INSIDE IS AMAZING !!! NOT ONLY MINE, TOM'S WORK BUT THE WORK OF ANOTHER GREAT ARTIST : GON'L. Gon'l is the artist persona of Rich Long. He is not only a GREAT ARTIST BUT A PERSONAL FRIEND I HAVE THE OPPORTUNITY TO LIST HIM AS A FRIEND BUT HE ALSO UNDERSTANDS ART LIKE I DO !!!! The drawing is again of a closeup of the building.

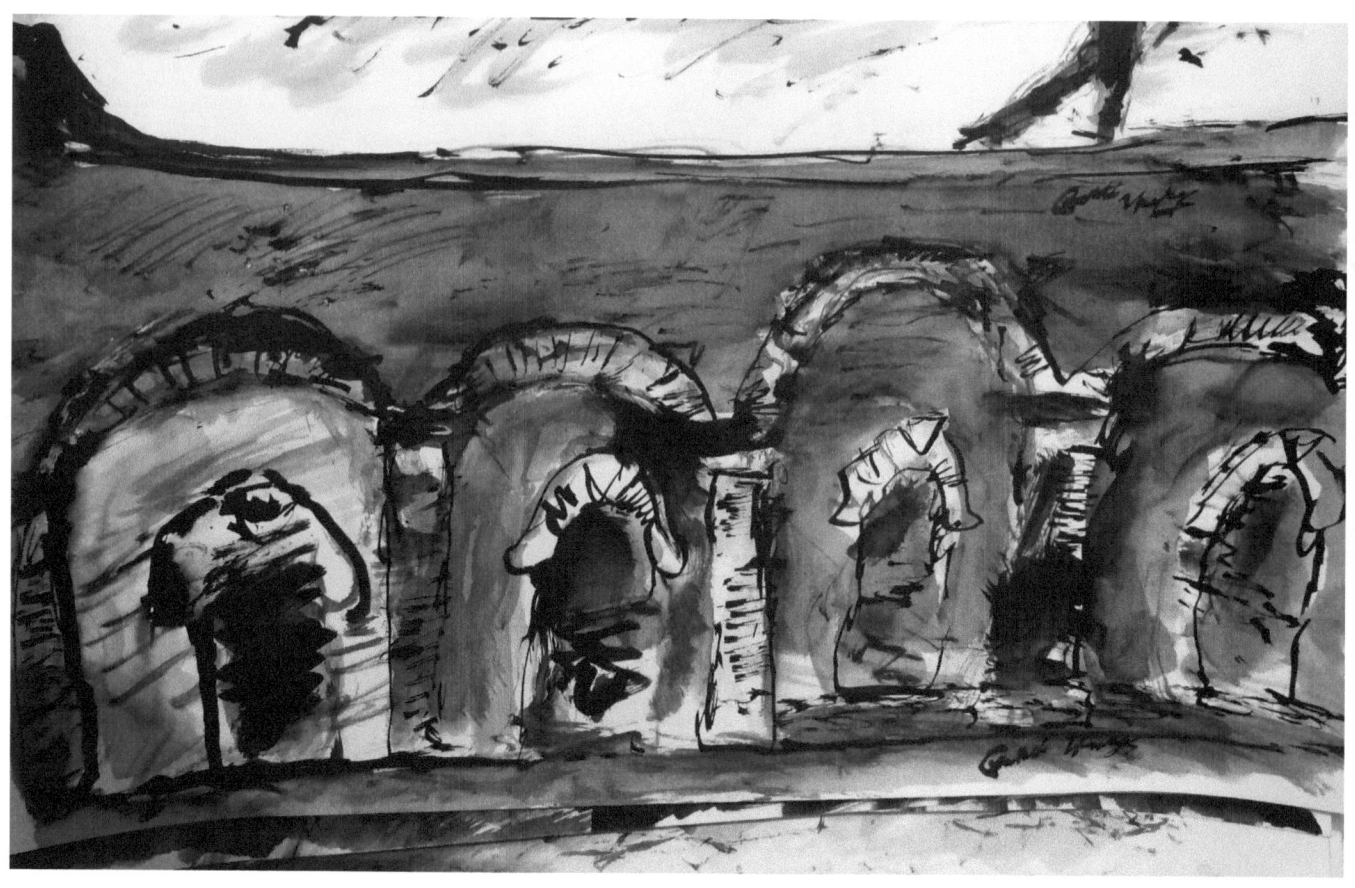

Figure 14- NEXT PAGE- now for some food. The following image is of a local establishment. Vinny's Stock Pot restaurant. This local restaurant is very good. The building is interesting as well. I would recommending eating here if you get to Bay City.

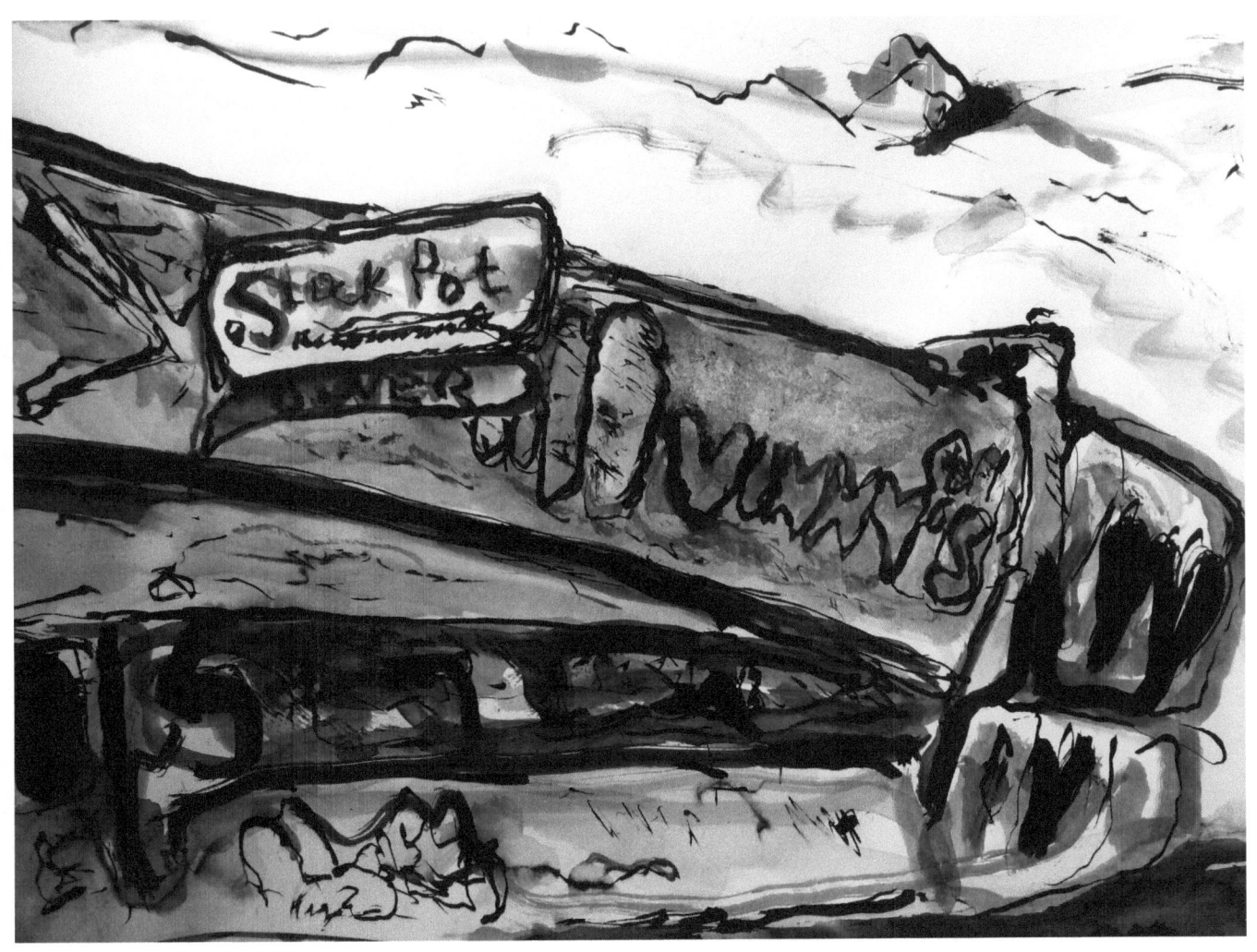

Figure 15- NEXT PAGE– this drawing is is of another local food establishment: Caris Red Lion Diner. This restaurant is mainly known for its breakfast especially omelets. The drawing give me an impression of the Nighthawks by Edward Hopper. I would be honored to be in the same company as Edward Hopper. But one of the main differences is that my drawing does not contain any people it is JUST A BUILDING. BUT IT IS JUST A GOOD DRAWING (AT LEAST I HOPE) !!!!!

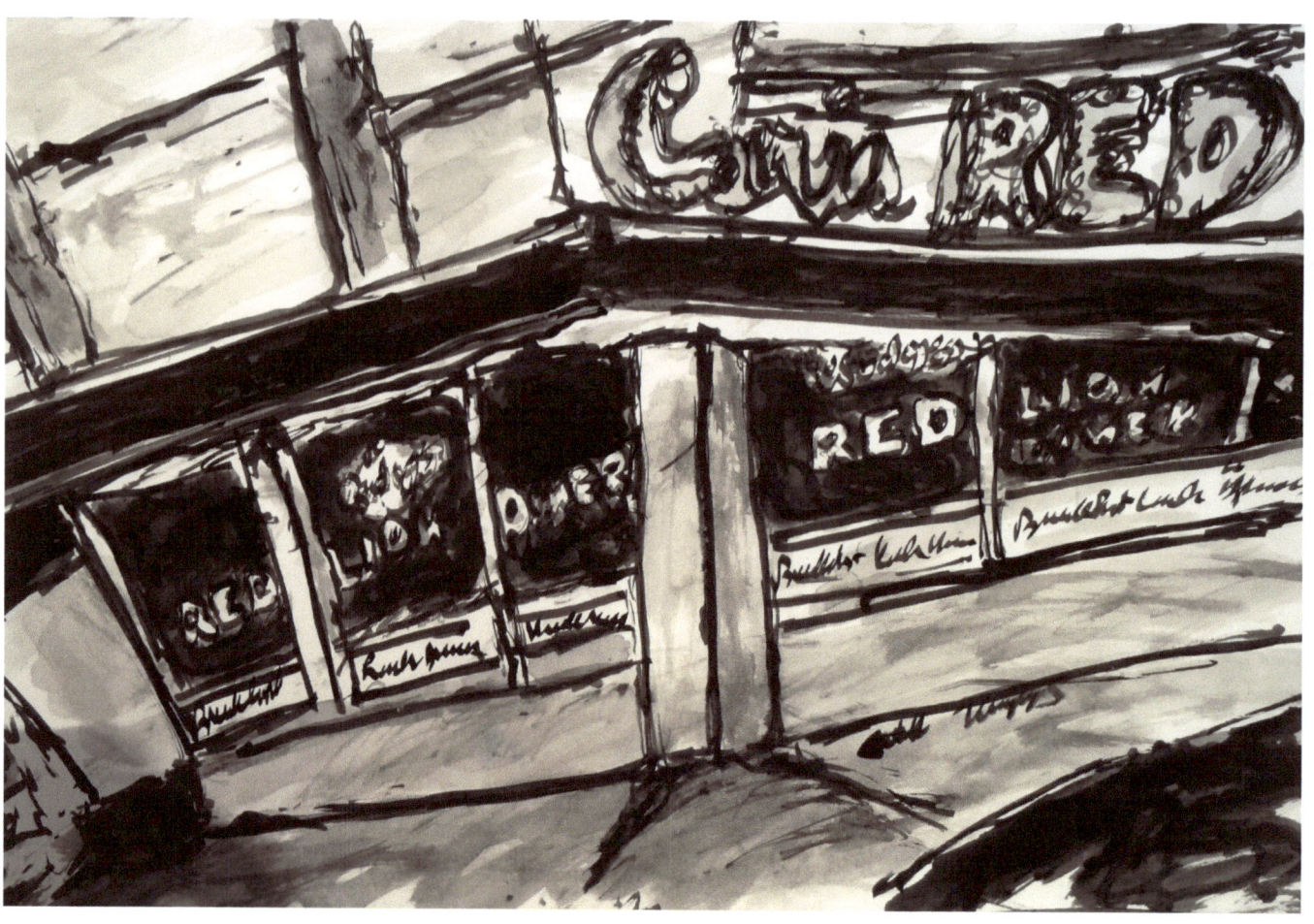

Figure 16- NEXT PAGE – the next 7 drawings are of historical houses of Bay City, four of these being on Center Avenue. The first building is of 710 Center Avenue . This house was built in 1876. ISN'T THE BUILDING'S ARCHITECTURE GREAT !!! This particular drawing is one of my favorite !! IT IS ONE OF MY MOST SUCCESSFUL ONES IN THIS BOOK !!!

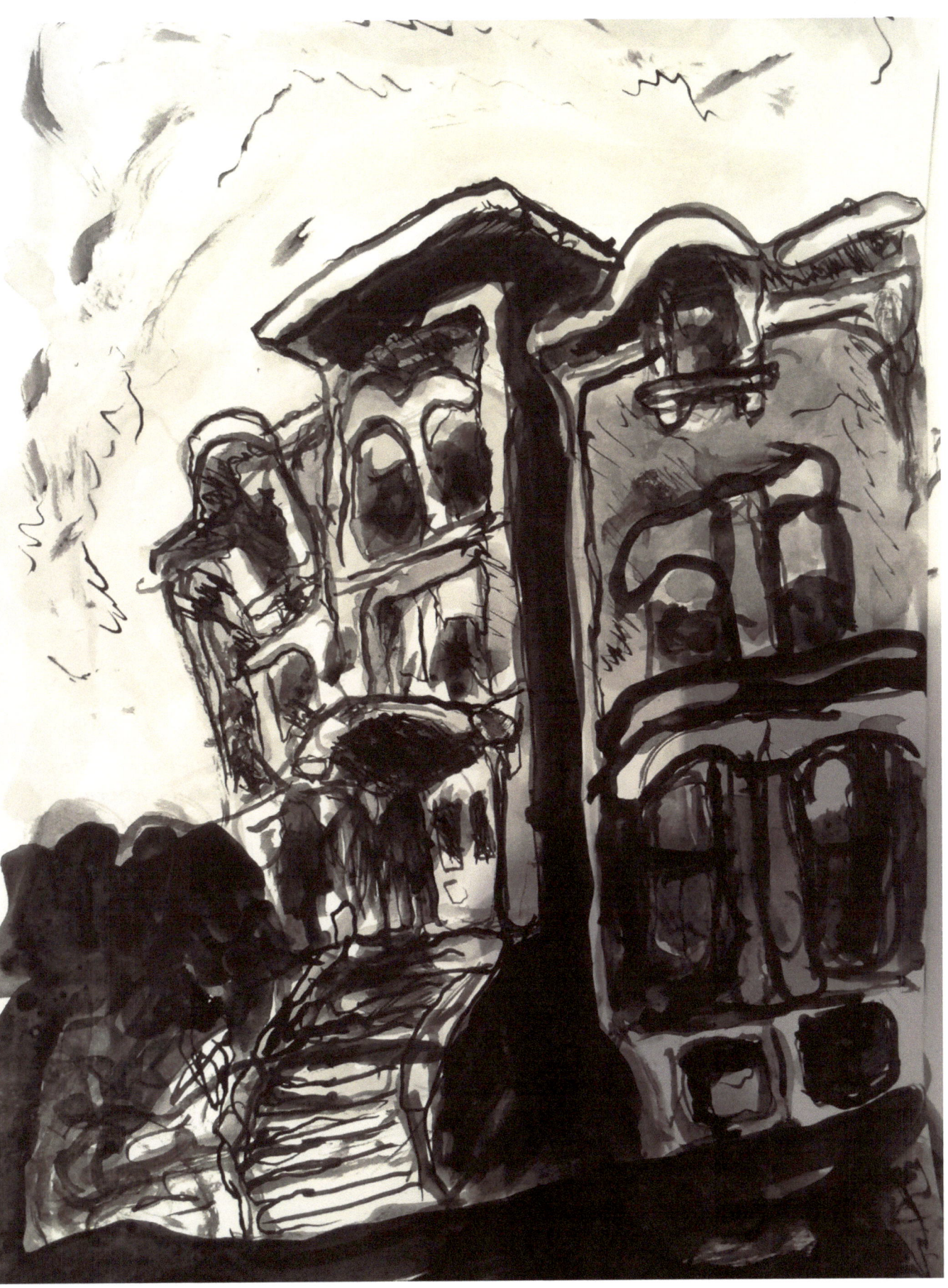

BUILDING OF IMPORTANCE

Figure 17 -NEXT PAGE- this building is old, built in 1891. It is not listed in the files of historical building\s but it holds some personal HISTORY for me !! IT is where currently live !!! On first glance it is of just an ordinary building but what makes it EXTRAORDINARY IS THAT IT IS WHERE I LIVE !!! IT IS WHERE MOST OF THE DRAWINGS FROM WHICH THAT BOOK WAS CREATED !!!

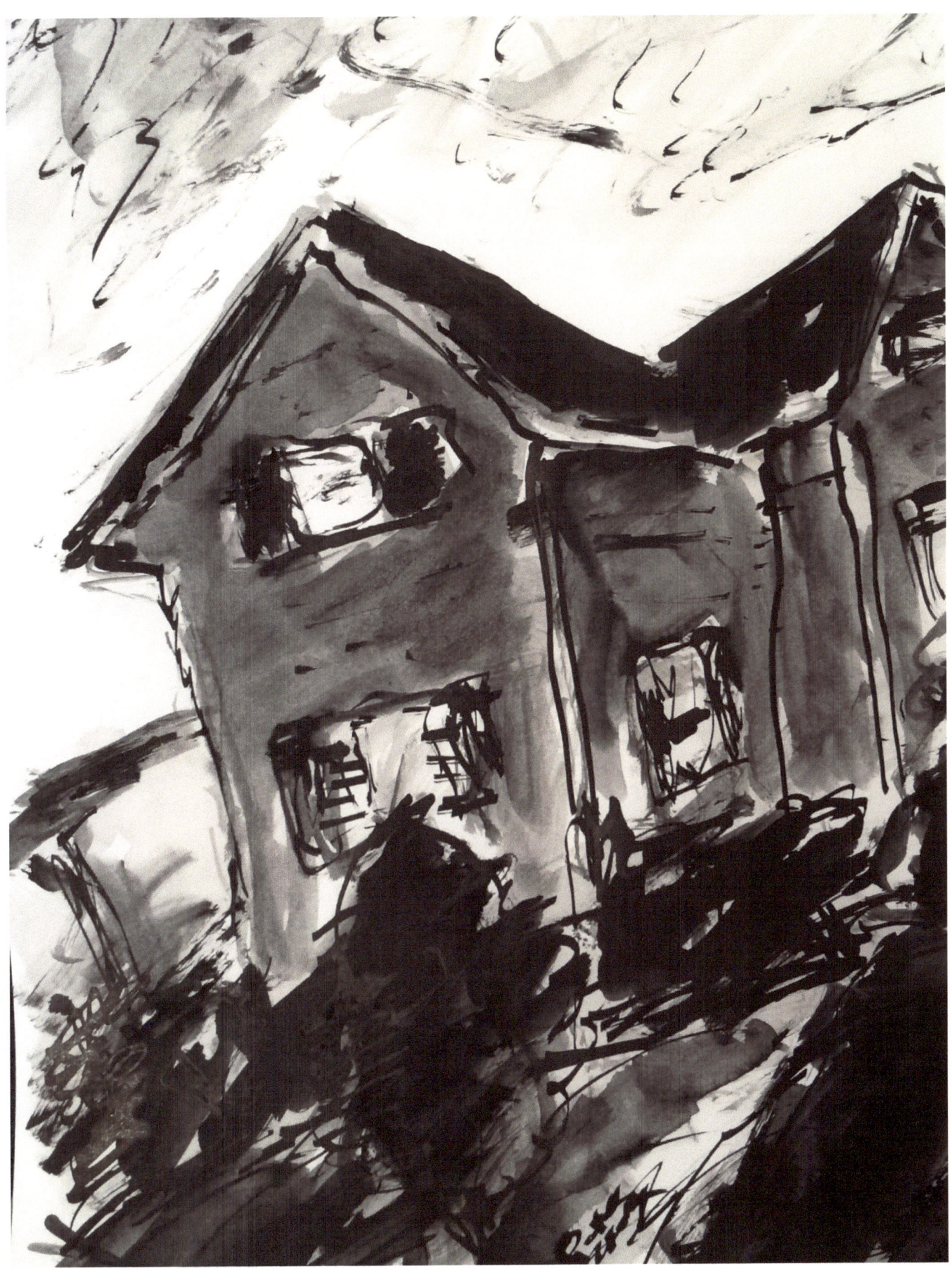

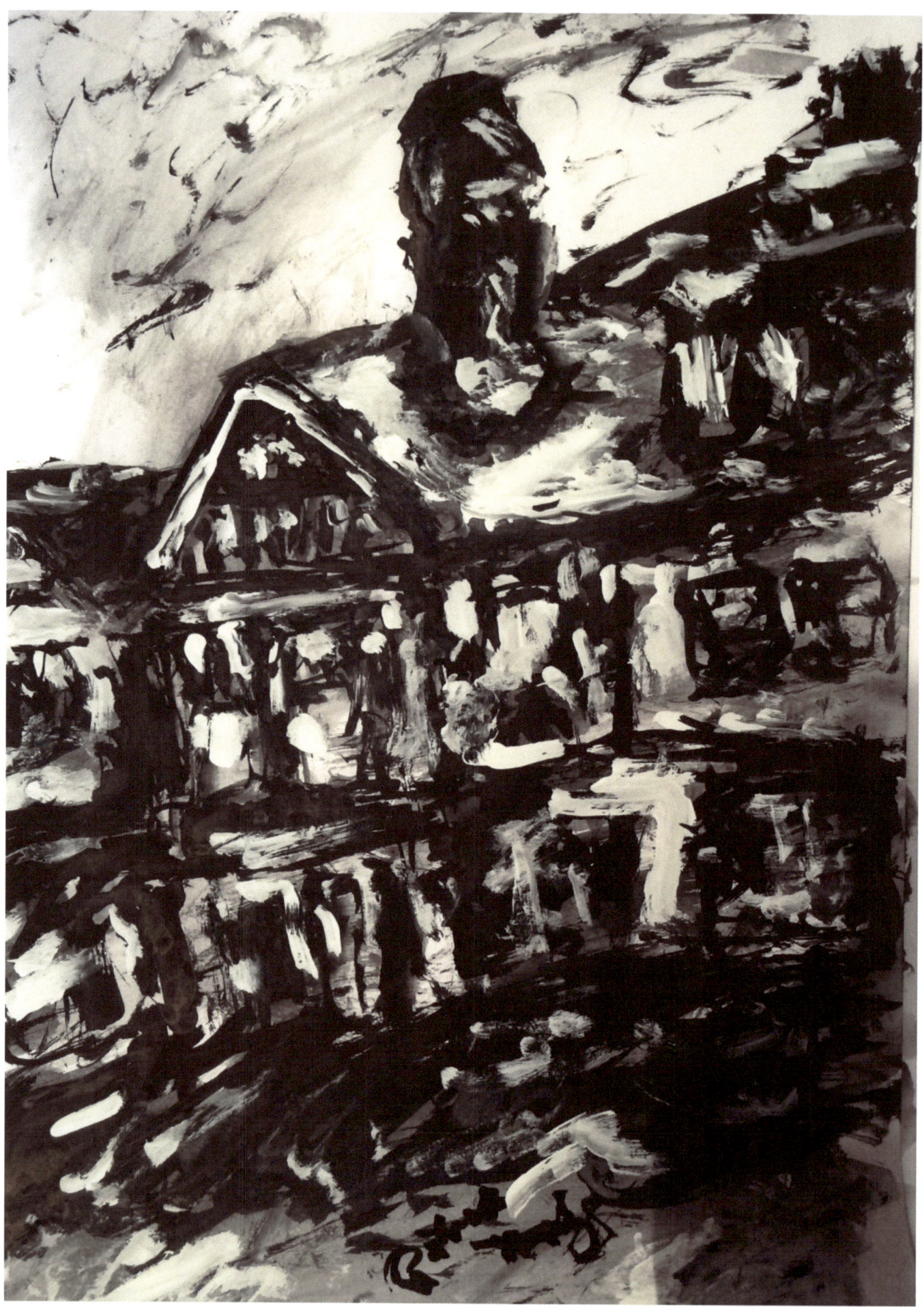

Figure 18- PREVIOUS PAGE- this image is of the house located at 206 West Midland Avenue in Bay City. This building was constructed in 1889. This drawing is a little more abstract than most of the other images. The drawing got too "dark" . I had to "lighten" it up with white acrylic paint. With the inclusion of the white paint , I breathed "life" back into this drawing. DO YOU AGREE ??

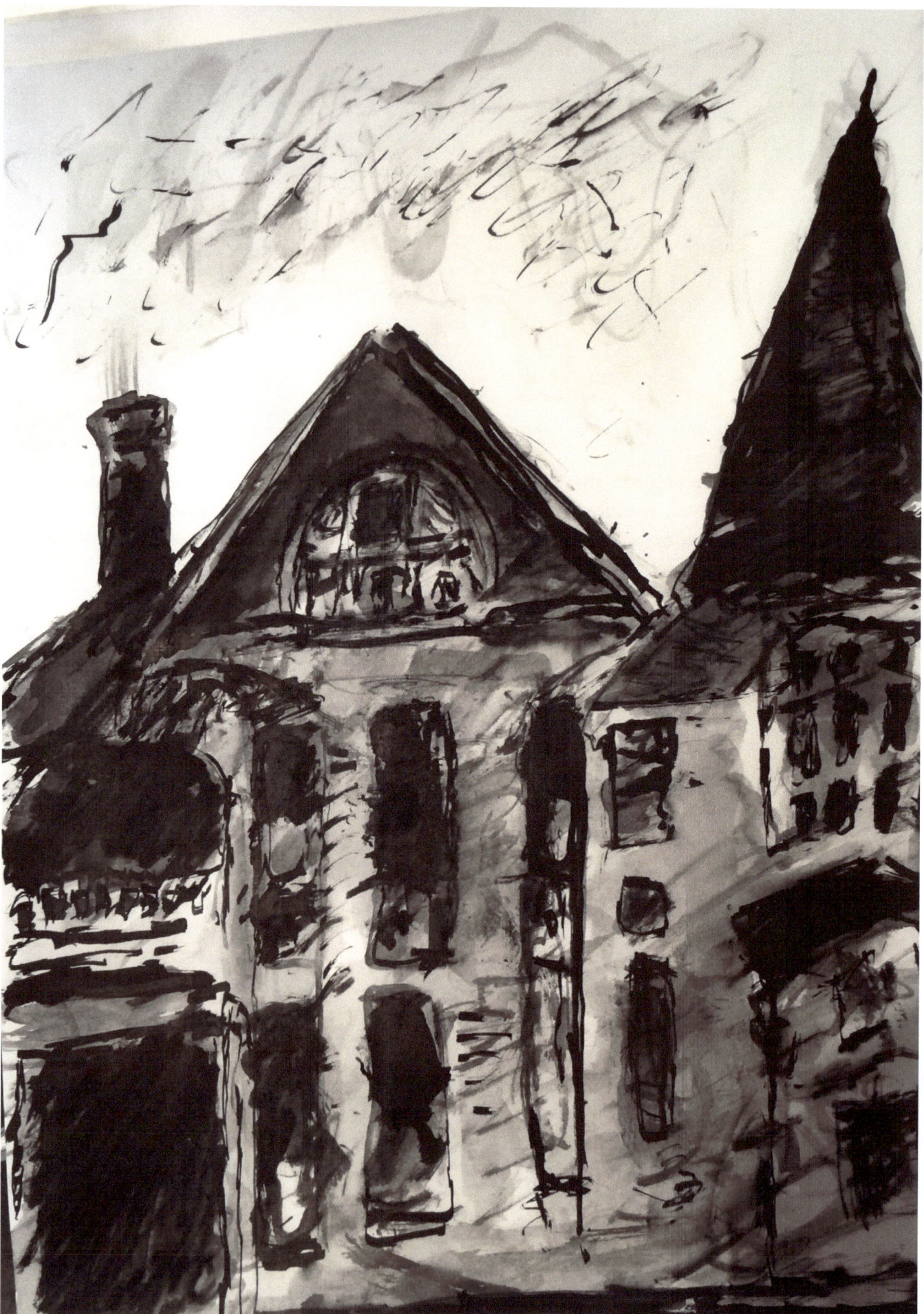

Figure 19- PREVIOUS PAGE- this building is again located on Center Avenue : 1315 Center Avenue . This building was constructed in 1887. Most of the really interesting buildings in Bay City were built around 1890 give or take a few years. THIS WAS A GREAT DECADE FOR ARCHITECTURE IN BAY CITY. The manner in which I painted this image is very expressive. The chimney looks like it is emitting smoke in the atmosphere. It gives the building "life". It is "breathing" so to speak. LET IT BREATHE FREELY IN THE BAY CITY SKY !!

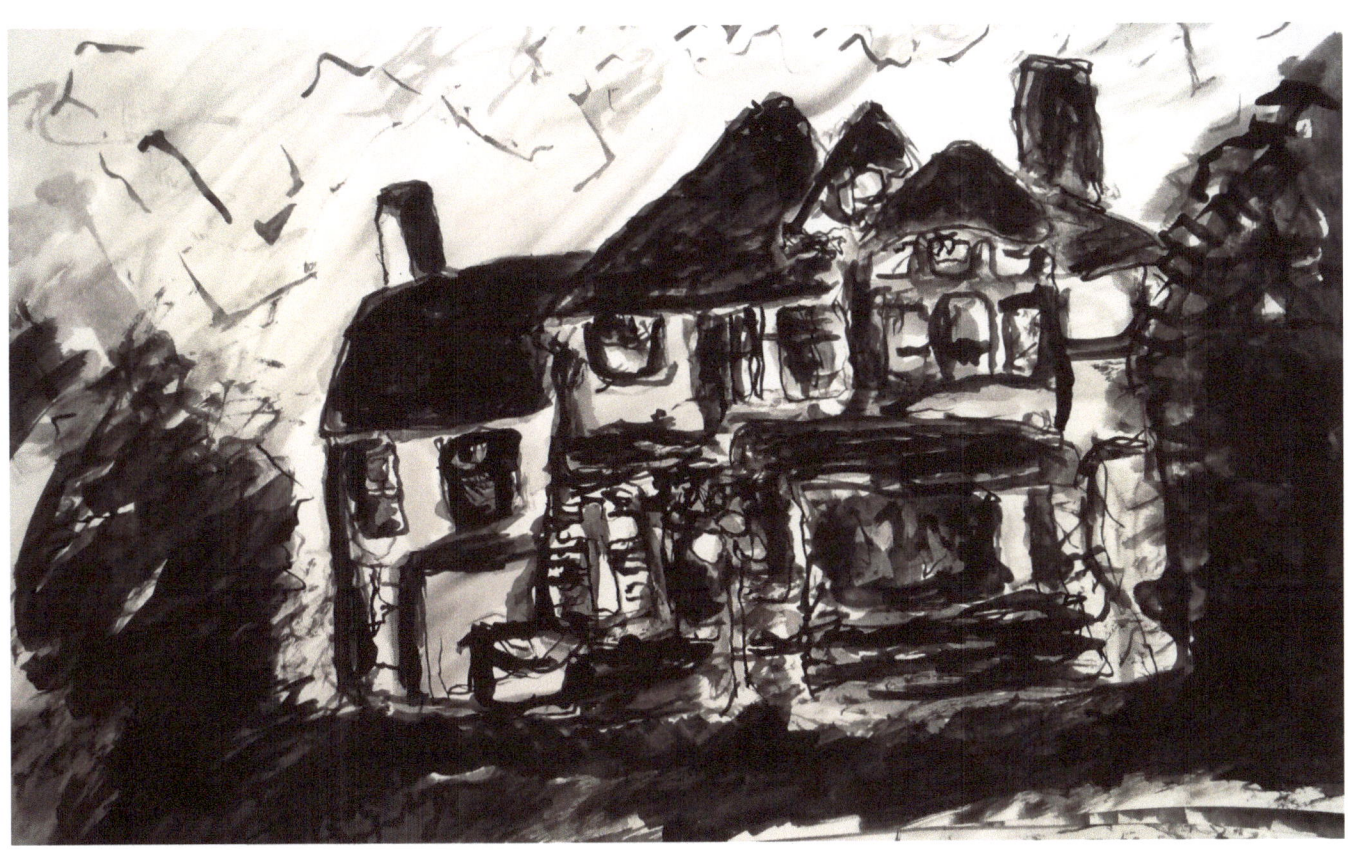

Figure 20 -ABOVE- this image is of yet another house on Center Avenue. The address of this building is 1712 Center. This building was again built in the 1890's: 1887 to be exact. The main difference between this image and many of the prior ones is that is is of the complete building. The whole building is portrayed with indications of trees around the structure. I DON'T THINK THIS DRAWING IS AS SUCCESSFUL AS MANY OF THE OTHERS. THE CLOSEUP OF BUILDINGS "WORK" BETTER !!

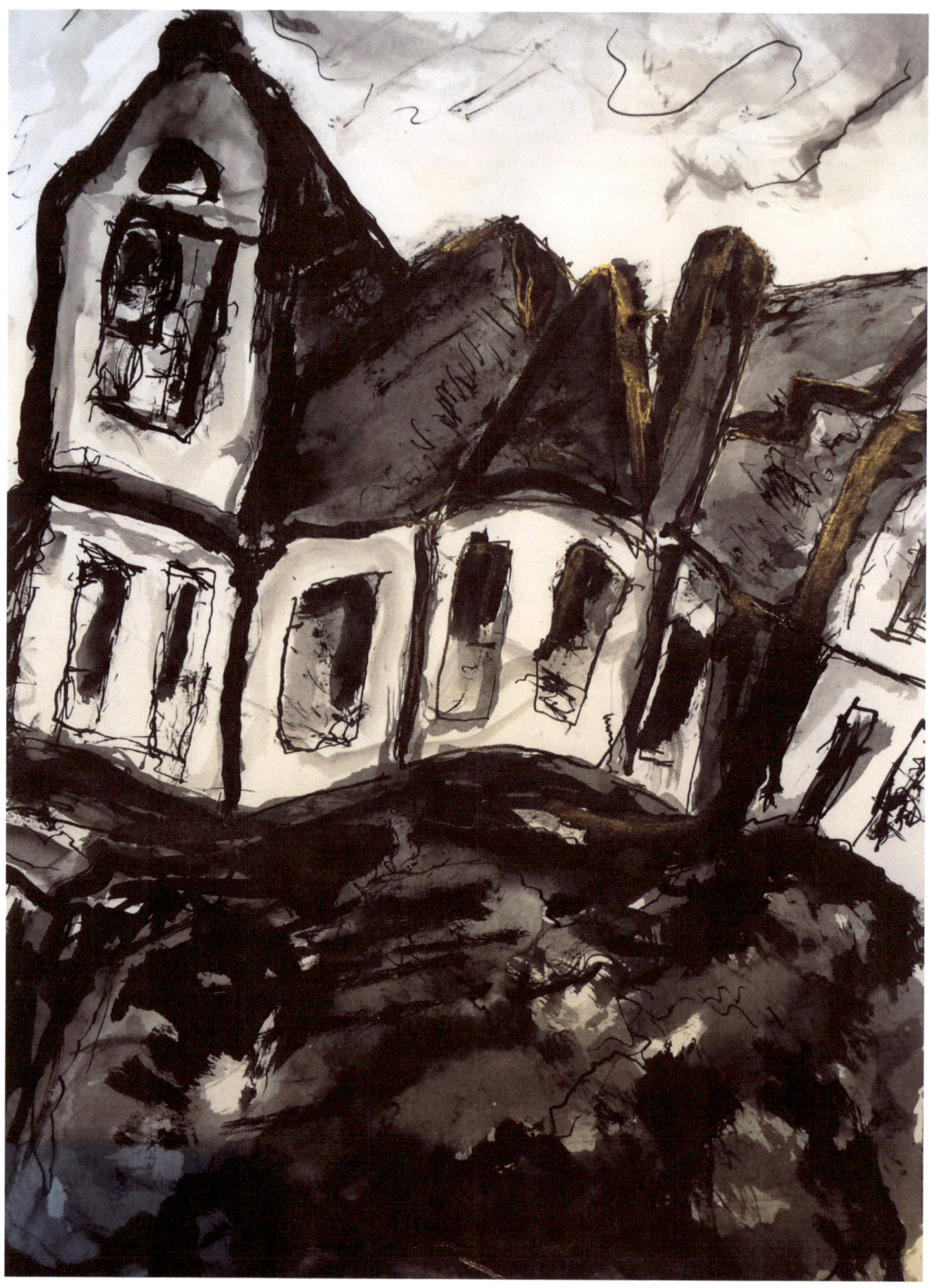

Figure 21- PREVIOUS PAGE- this image is of another building on Center Avenue. This time the building is located at 1515 Center Avenue with a construction date near 1890, 1891 to be exact. This building seems to be "moving". The manner of which I painted it gives the viewer the impression of "movement". It is reminiscent of the landscape paintings of Chaim Soutine- my favorite painter of all time !! The building appears to be " swaying" .

Figure 22- NEXT PAGE- this last image of a house is located at 400 North Walnut Street and was built in 1883. Yet another building from the era of 1890. This drawing I REALLY LIKE !! THIS ONE IS VERY SUCCESSFUL !! THIS IS PROBABLY ONE OF MY FAVORITE ONES I CREATED. THE MANNER OF WHICH I PAINTED THE ROUND PORTION OF THE BUILDING WORKS "GOOD". WHAT DO YOU THINK !?!

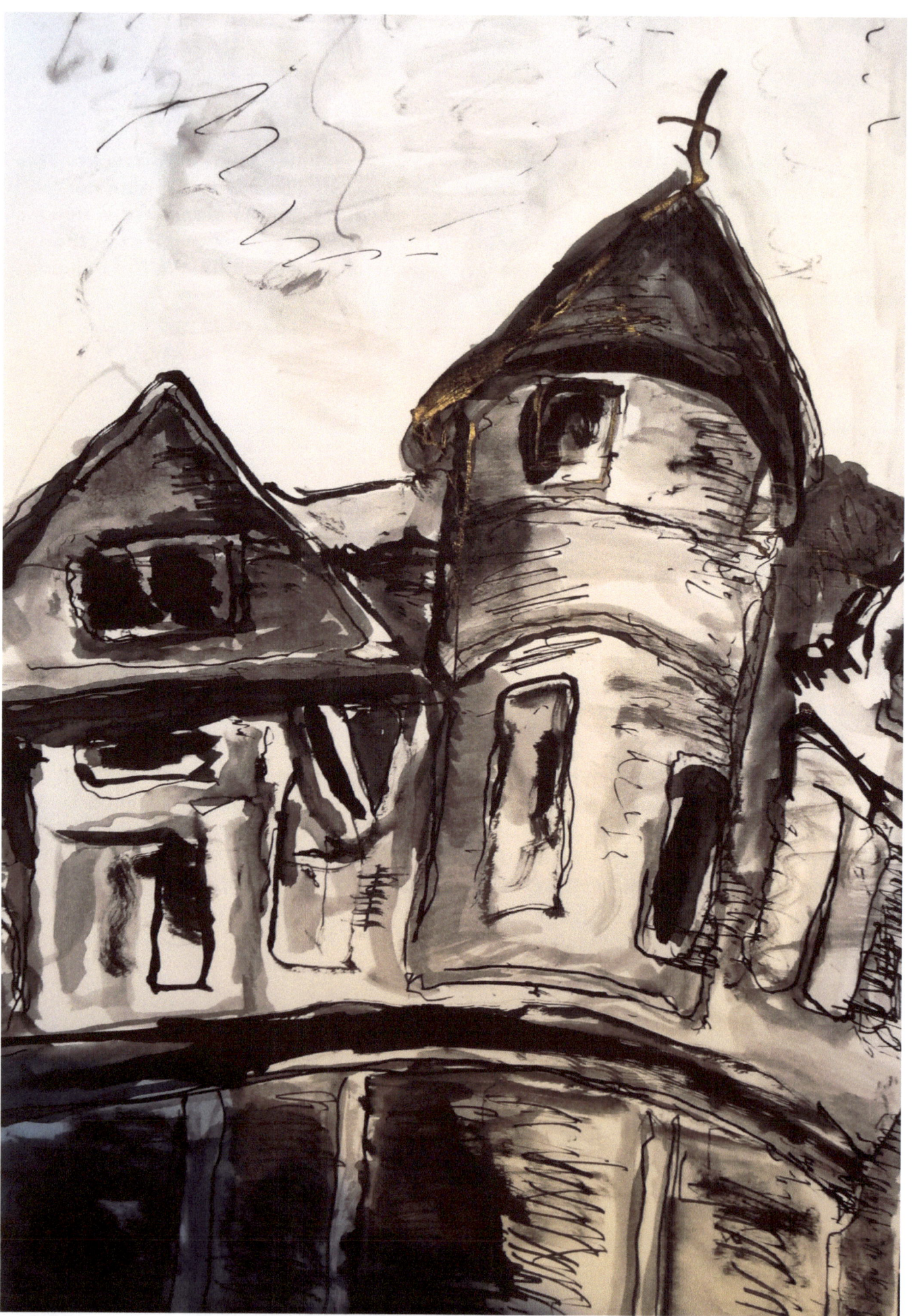

THE NEXT SIX IMAGES ARE OF CHURCHES IN BAY CITY

THE CHURCHES OF BAY CITY

Figure 23- O-gua-kawning Church- Native American- NOT USED AS CHURCH TODAY
Figure 24- Saint Stanislaus Kostka Church- CATHOLIC
Figure 25- First Baptist Church- BAPTIST
Figure 26- First Presbyterian Church- PRESBYTERIAN
Figure 27- Trinity Episcopal Church- EPISCOPAL
Figure 28- Westminister Presbyterian Church- PRESBYTERIAN

THIS IS BUT A SMALL SAMPLING OF THE CHURCHES OF BAY CITY. THERE ARE MANY MANY CHURCHES IN BAY CITY. THE ONLY THING THAT THERE IS MORE OF IN BAY CITY ARE BARS. CHURCHES AND BARS !!??!! WHAT DOES THAT MEAN !!??!!!

Figure 23- NEXT PAGE- this image is of the oldest church building in Bay City. IT IS NO LONGER IN USE TODAY. It is a Native American Church with a name that I can not pronounce: O-gua-kawning Church. This churches has a historical marker outside that proudly displays its heritage. I "pray" I did it justice with my drawing . What do you think ??

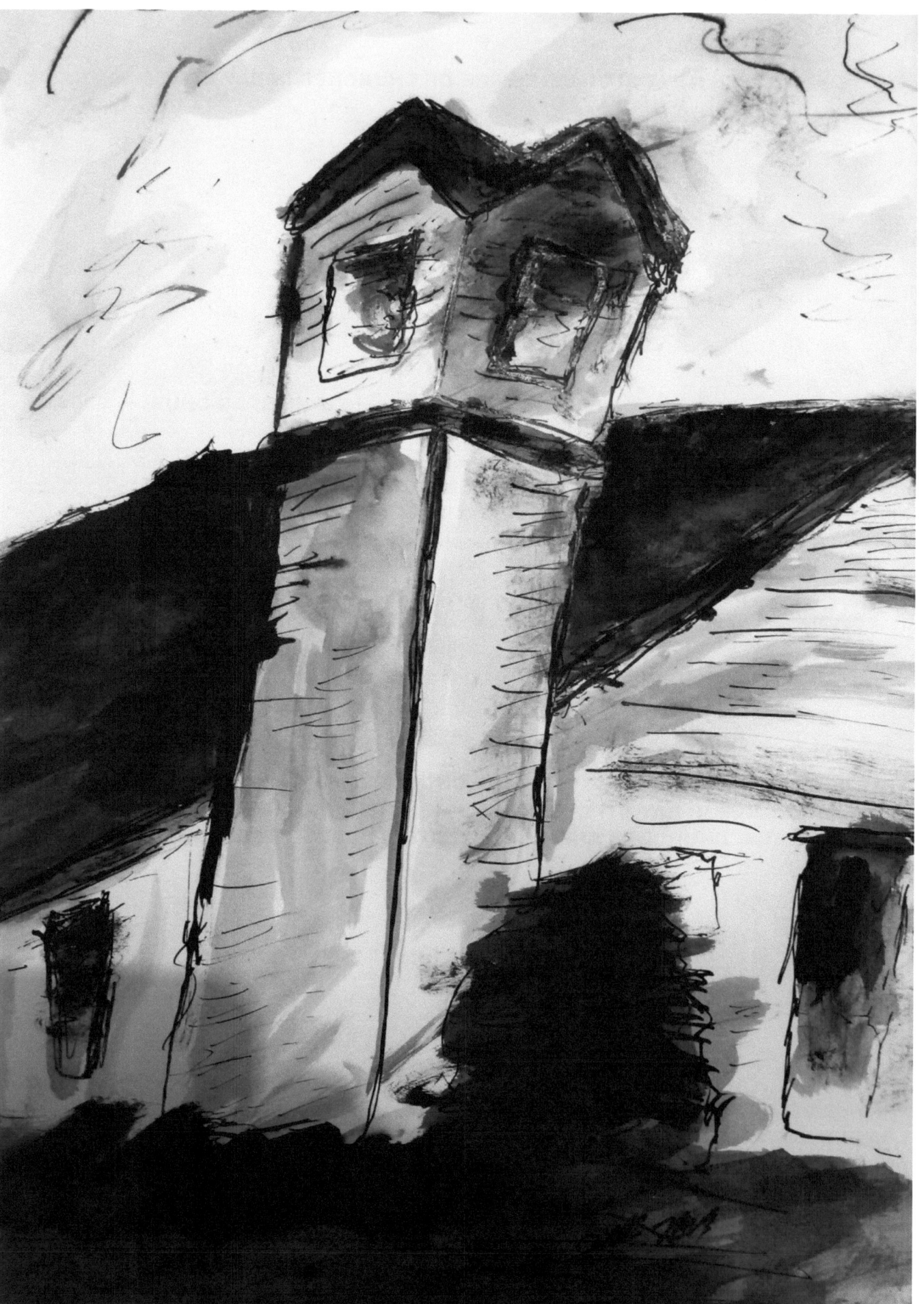

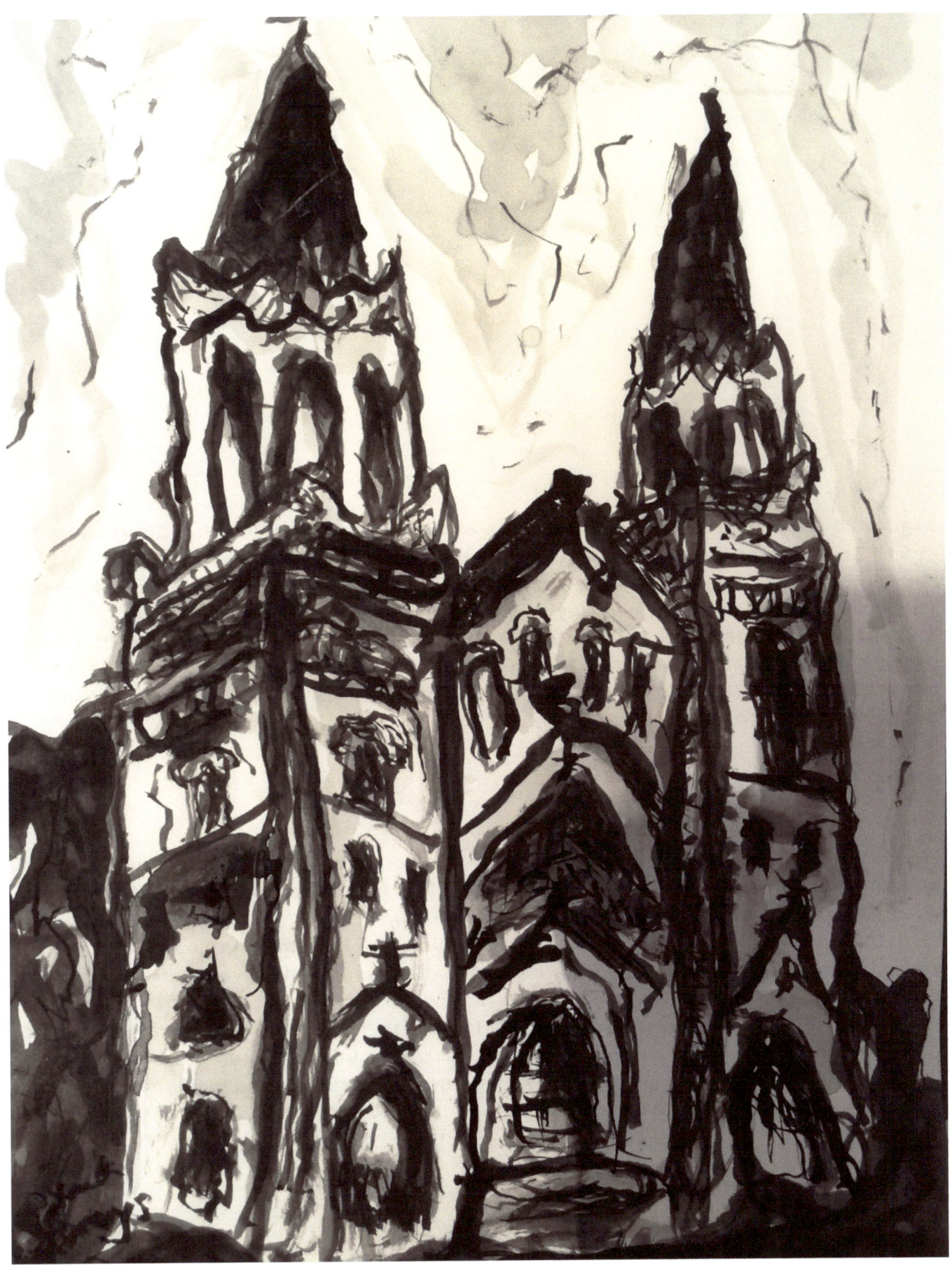

Figure 24- PREVIOUS PAGE- this image is of Saint Stanislaus Kostka Church located at 915 South Grant Street. This beautiful building was constructed in 1892. This church illustrates two major things in Bay City. Polish people and Catholic Churches. There are both of abundance in Bay City. MANY POLISH PEOPLE AND MANY CATHOLIC CHURCHES !!!! THIS DRAWING IS ONE OF THE MOST SUCCESSFUL ONES IN THIS BOOK. TOM LARSON REALLY THINKS THIS DRAWING "WORKS". I VALUE HIS OPINION AND I AGREE WITH HIM. OF ALL THE DRAWINGS I HAVE DONE THIS ONE GETS THE MOST FAVORABLE REVIEW. WHAT DO YOU THINK ??

Figure 25- NEXT PAGE- this image is of a church very similar to Saint Stanislaus. The building has two towers just like Saint Stans. The church located in Bay City at 1145 West Center Avenue is First Baptist Church . Actually it is in Essexville. This Church as depicted in my image seems like it is in motion, the building seems to be on the verge of "moving". Just like the paintings of landscapes by my favorite artist : Chaim Soutine. His feverish brush strokes in the landscape make it appear to be "alive" just like this image the towers appear to be just about to "move". The quivering lines and the nervous brushstrokes convey this sentiment. This image I think is a strong one like the Saint Stans . They both are reminiscent of paintings done by Monet of churches in France. What a great comparison !!!! I WOULD LOVE TO BE COMPARED TO MONET !!!!

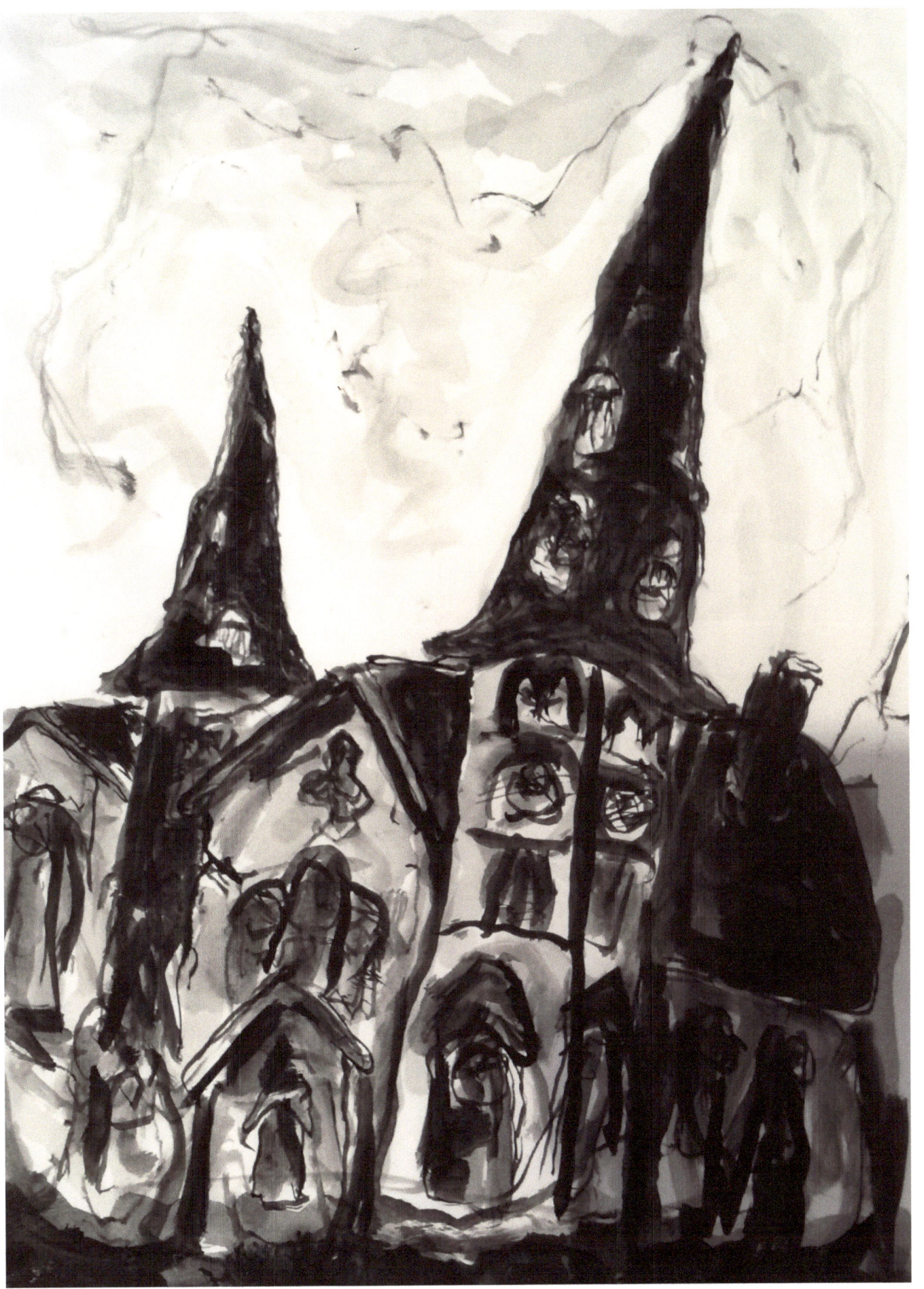

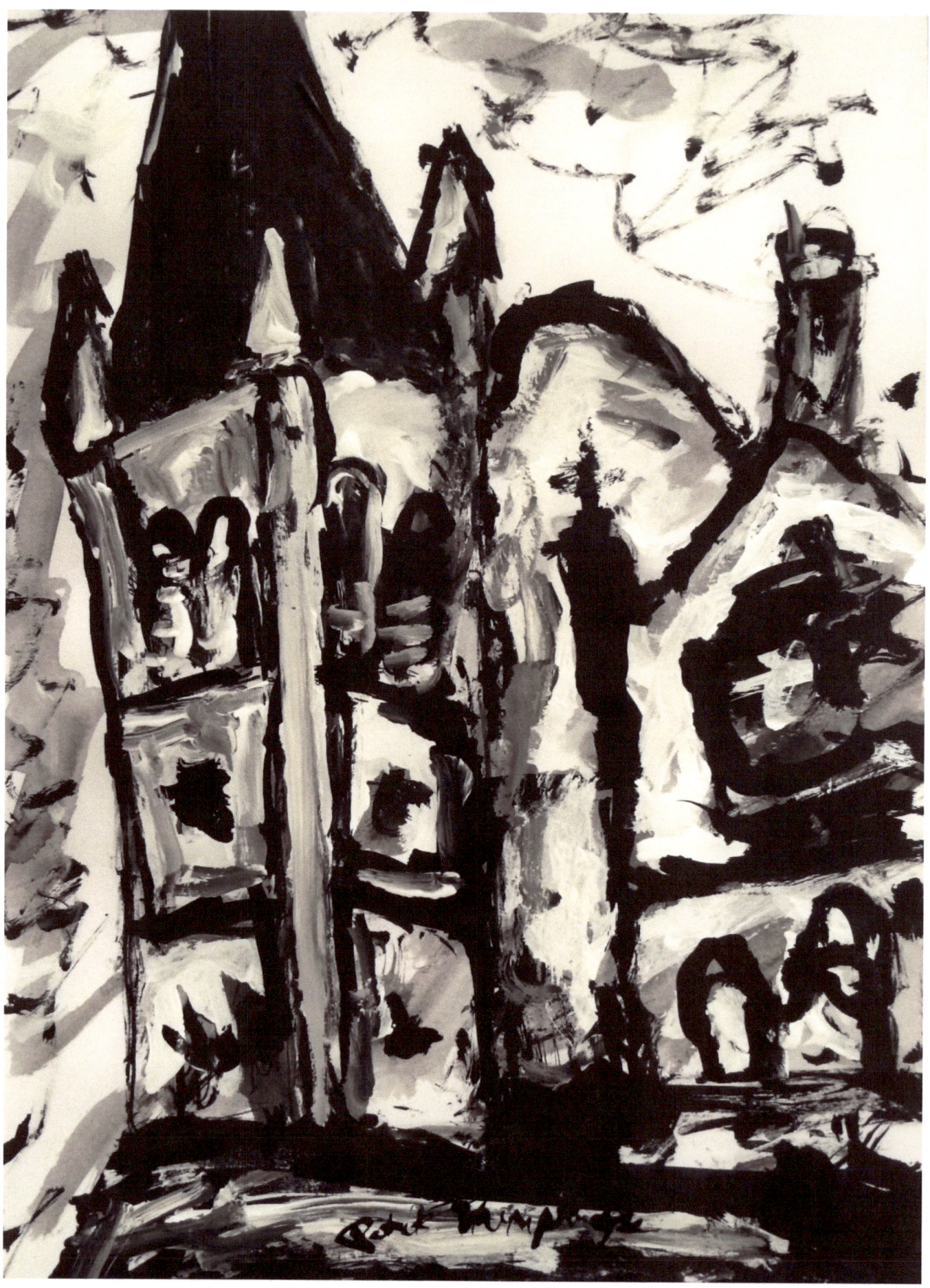

Figure 26 -PREVIOUS PAGE- this image is of another great church of Bay City. This church is First Presbyterian Church at 805 Center Avenue. This church was constructed in 1893. This painting contains white acrylic paint because the painting got too "dark". The white acrylic paint "saved" the image just like the church member that attends here "saves" their soul.

Figure 27-NEXT PAGE- this church is different from the previous two : it contains one main tower instead of two. This church located at 911 Center Avenue is Trinity Episcopal Church built in 1887. Trinity meaning "three" but the building itself has but "one" tower: one true faith . One true belief. Just like Jesus is the "one". There is "one" single tower that reaches up to Heaven . Do you believe ?

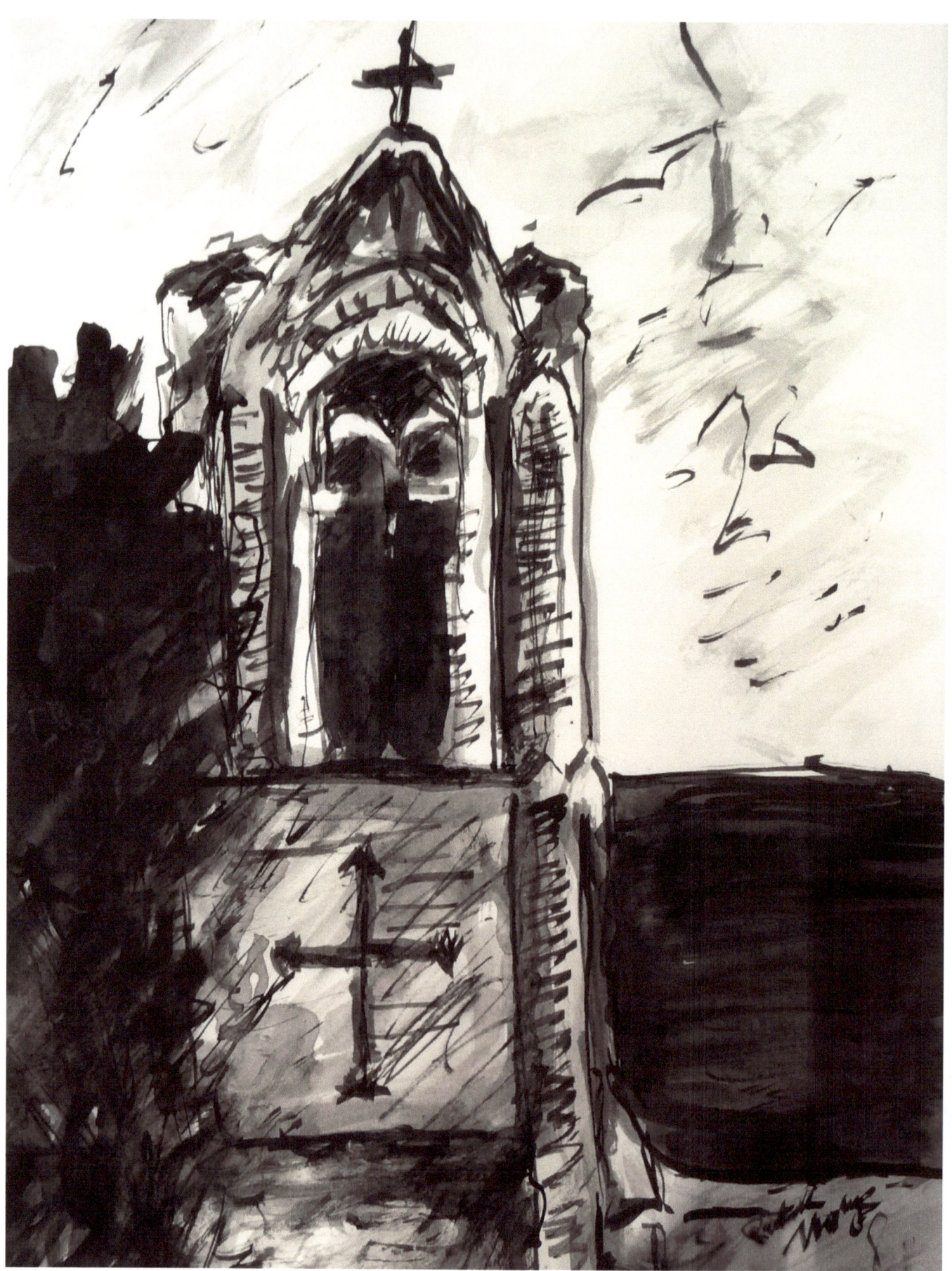

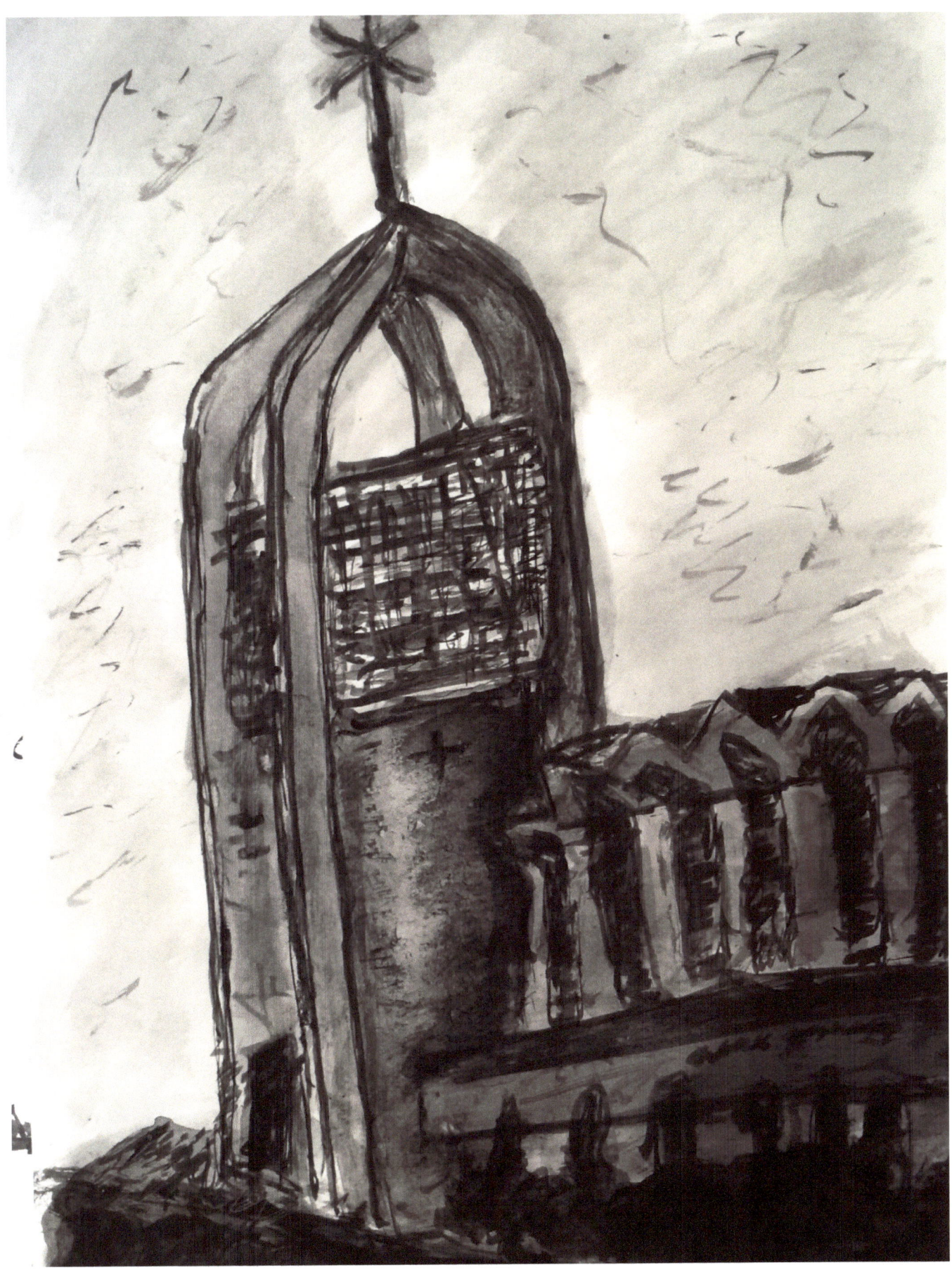

Figure 28-PREVIOUS PAGE- this last church is Westminister Presbyterian Church located at 103 East Midland Street. This building has the "unique" tower that can be seen from afar. The shaped cement holding the steel cage in the tower is very interesting. This particular church holds some "personal" history for me: I was married here in 1998. Unfortunately my marriage is not still "standing" but this church is still "standing". Just like God's love that eternally points with its tower towards Heaven. This church stands "forever" in the Bay City skyline.

NOW FOR SOMETHING DIFFERENT

Figure 29-NEXT PAGE- this image is of a different type of building that has a tower : a lighthouse. This particular lighthouse is the Old Saginaw River Lighthouse, 1876 , located in Bangor Township. The lighthouse was deactivated in 1960 and is currently being renovated . The lighthouse is not accessible to the public but it is "accessible" to many viewers. Amazing how many people identify with lighthouses. Do you find this image "accessible" ???

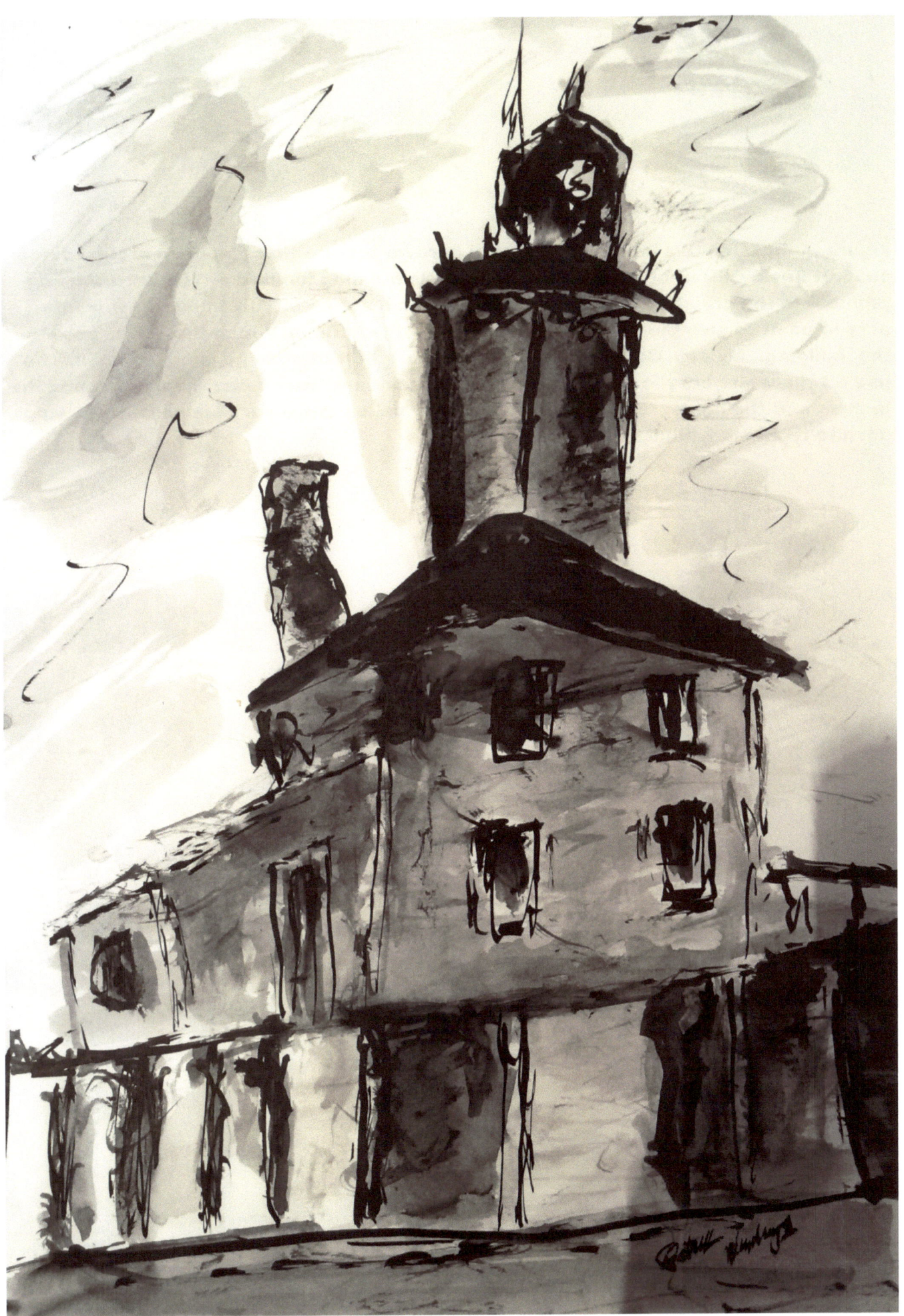

Figure 30-BELOW- this image is of a local hardware store that has been around since 1916. It has a "different" name Putz . This little building located at 201 Salzburg "shines" in the grey Bay City sky despite its peculiar name. This image I use white acrylic paint to give the impression of snow on the building which there was snow on the building. My son, Cameron , took the picture that this image is based upon. The use o f the white acrylic paint with the fine black lines from using the dip pen and the inclusion of the name "PUTZ" on the building makes this a very successful drawing despite its name ? What do you think ??

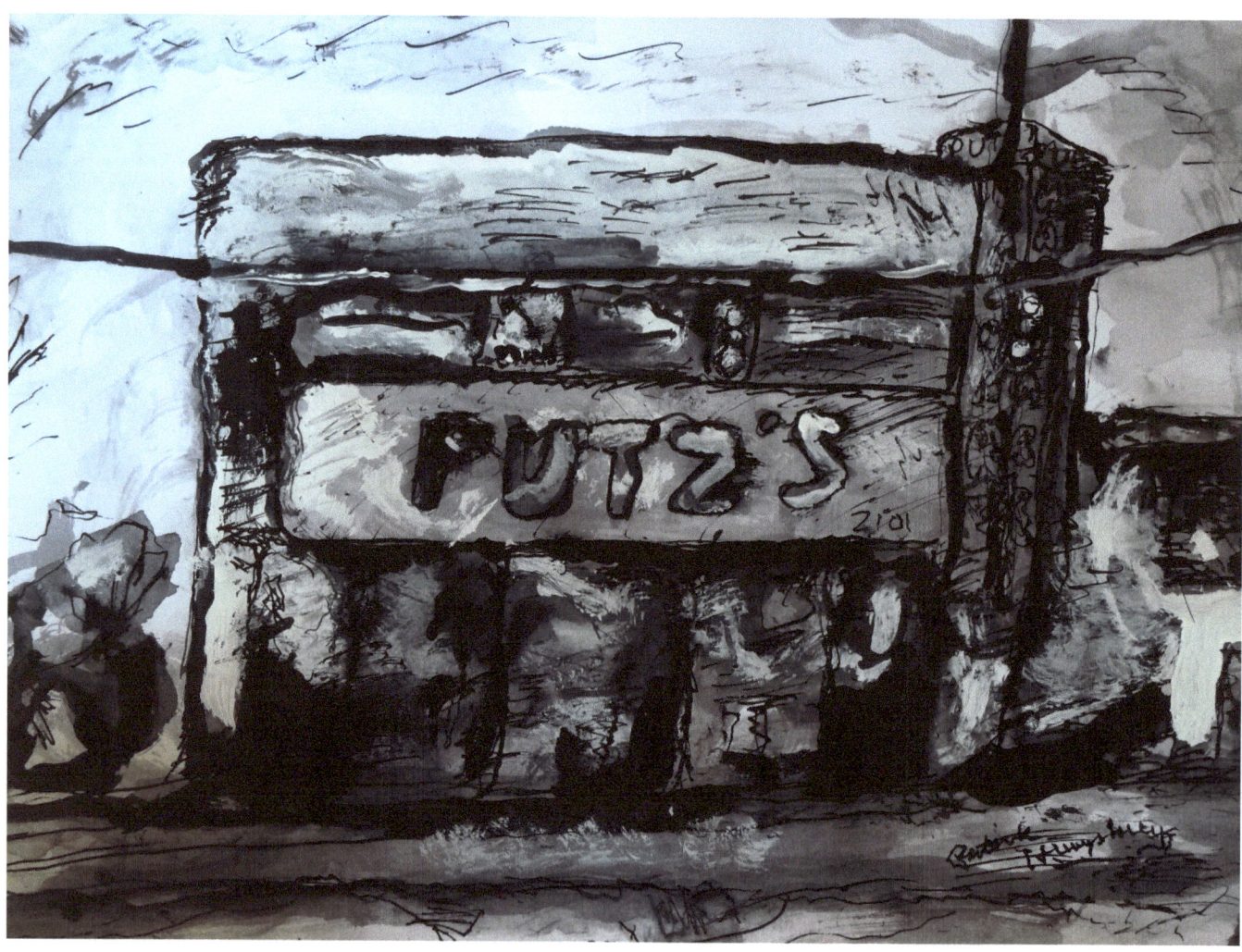

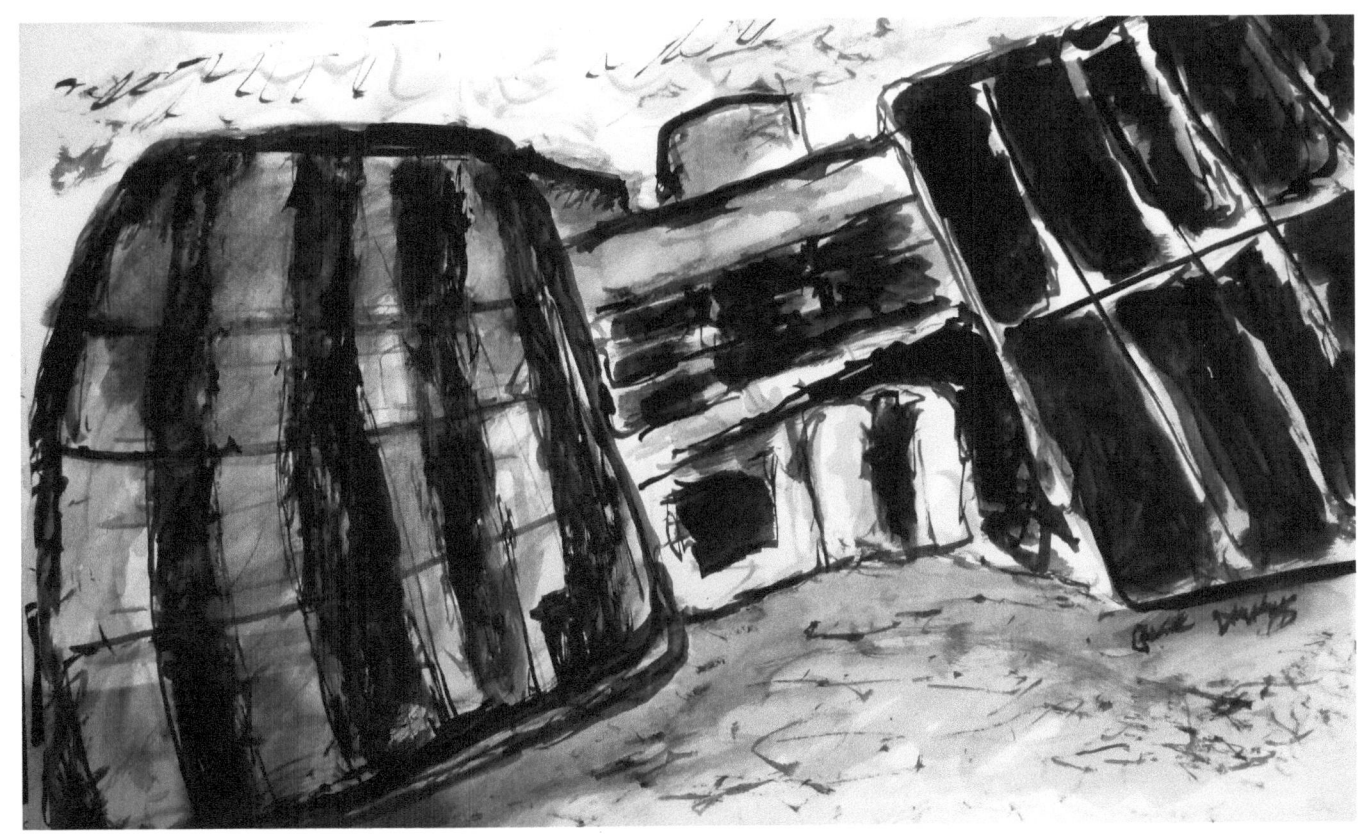

Figure 31- ABOVE- this image and the next one are of a very interesting building in Bay City . One that is "out of this world" literally !! It is the Delta College Planetarium. This building I like so much I did two drawings of it. The next drawing (figure 32) I think is more successful.

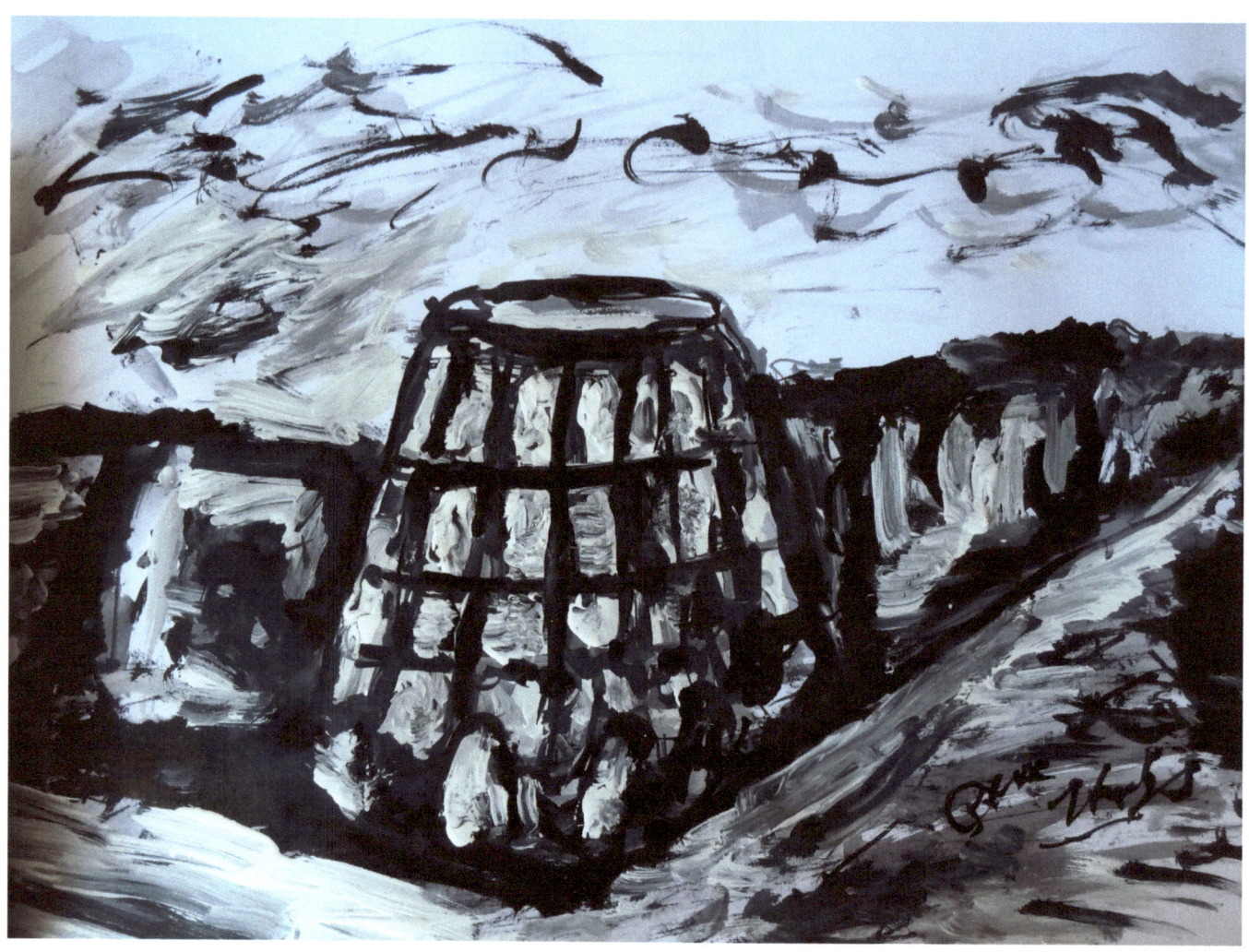

Figure 32-ABOVE- this is another drawing of that "out there" building that occupies the address at 100 Center Avenue in Bay City. This drawing uses white acrylic paint to "lighten" up some of the "dark" spots in the Bay City downtown. If you get a chance to take the "rocket" to Bay City let this destination be on   the "flight path" to Bay City!!! You won't regret it !!

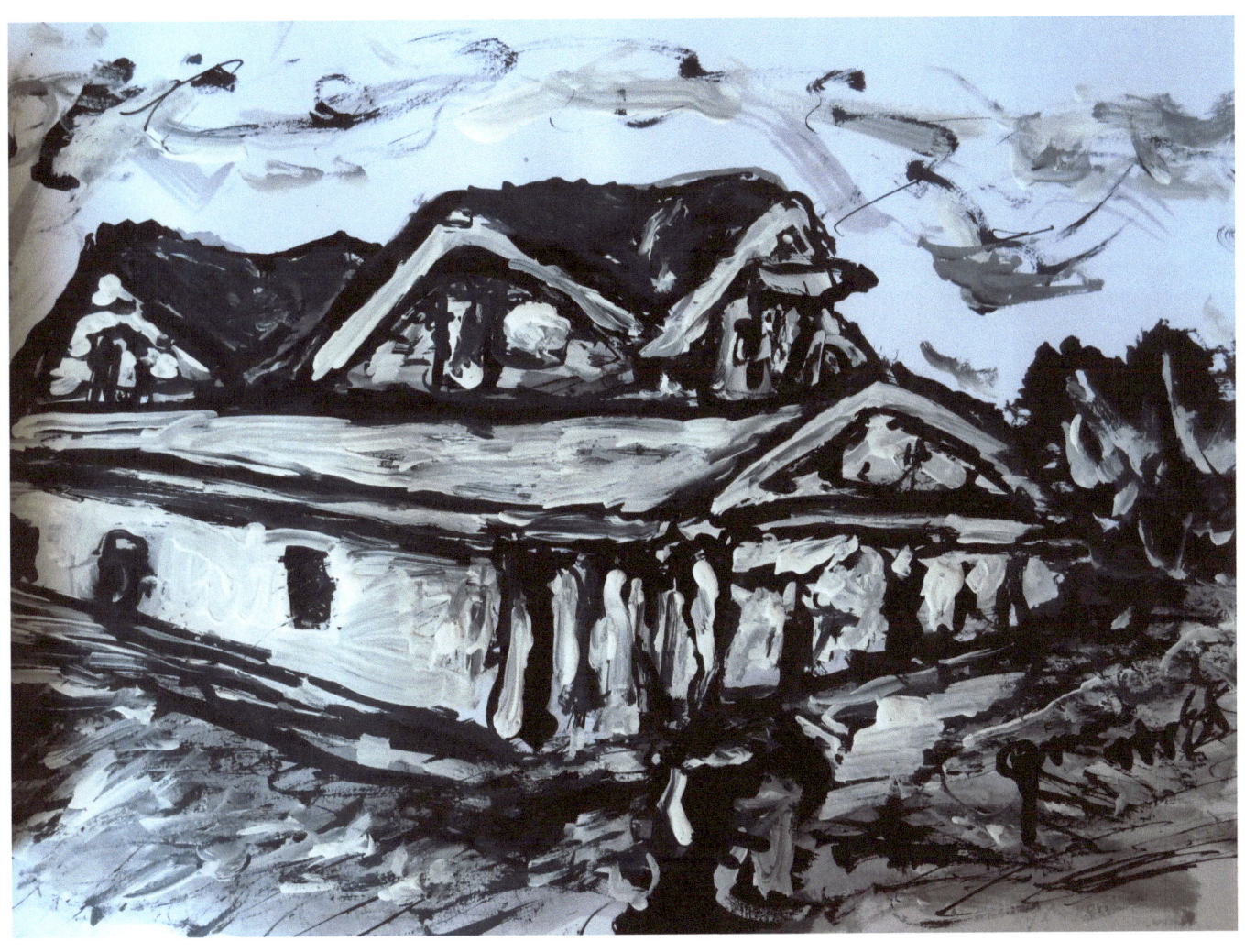

Figure 33- ABOVE- this image is of amazing building right by the Lafayette Bridge at 350 West Lafayette Avenue . This is one beautiful building !!! I have never been inside but the outside is phenomenal !! It isn't open during the grey days of winter . Just during the summer. This building houses the Bay City Rowing Club. My black and white drawing doesn't do it justice !!! The building is painted wonderfully !!! This building is my favorite one in Bay City !!! I will have to do a colored drawing of it ....

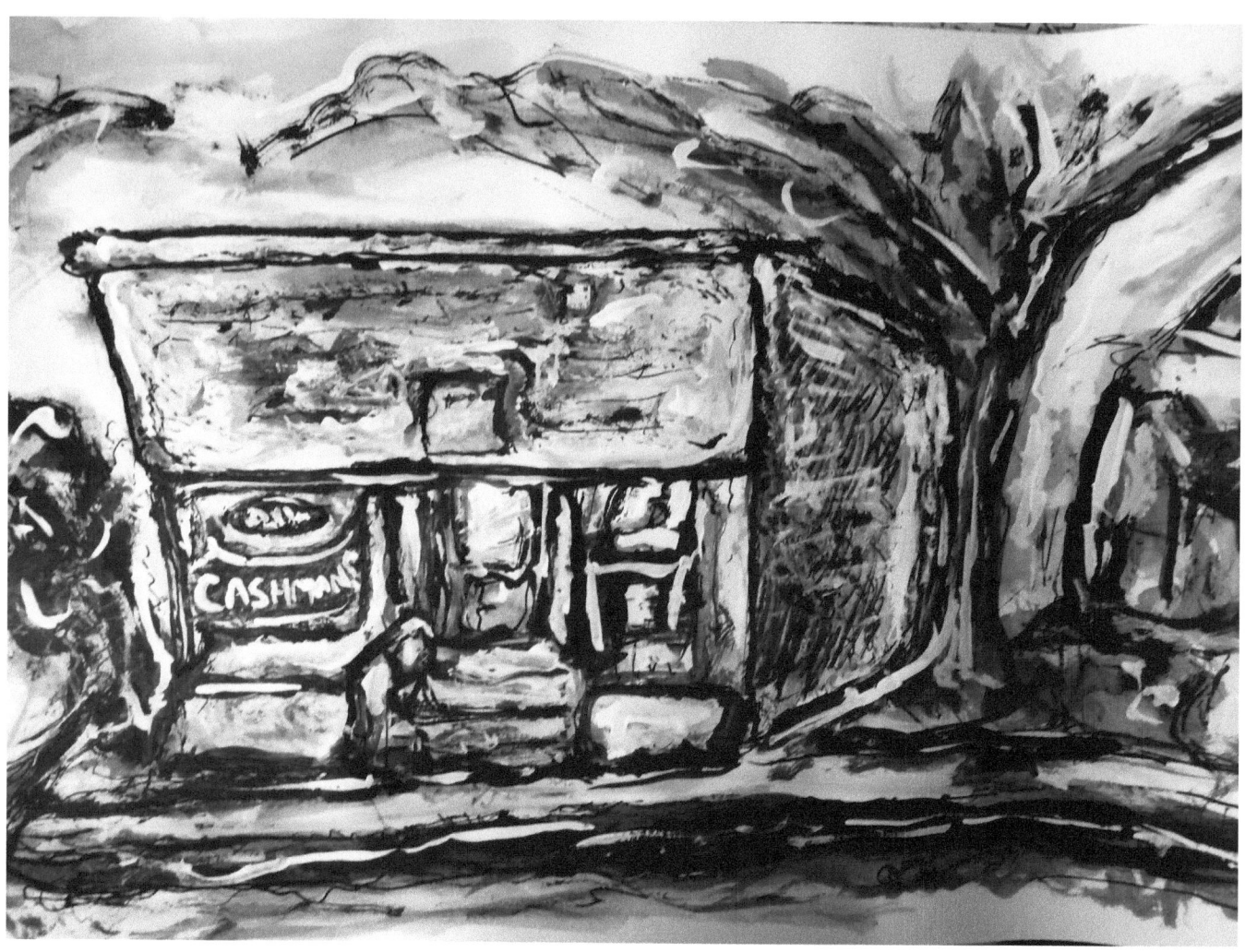

Figure 34 – ABOVE- this building "quietly" resides at 1018 South Madison Avenue in Bay City. This building is of Cashman's Comics. This local haven of comics has been "alive" for over 17 years. The manner of which I created this image gives it the feeling of "movement". The building "sways" in the winter wind. A good image to end the main part of my book about Bay City , Michigan buildings but "stick around" there are several images in the appendix !!

APPENDIX

This part of the book contains many things: book that inspired me, books I have also written, a couple of the drawings in color, a preview of my next book: an original comic book.

Book that started it all

Bay City : then and now, by Leon Kartzinger, ISBN: 978-0738533315, Arcadia Publishing, 2004.

My other books

(1)   Balinese Beckoning, CreateSpace, 2013, ISBN: 978-1494804770.
(2)   Broken Dreams, CreateSpace, 2013, ISBN: 978-1492734161.
(3)   Divorce Diary, CreateSpace, 2013, ISBN: 978-148030257.
(4)   Drawn to believe, CreateSpace, 2013, ISBN: 978-1490568621.
(5)   low key supermarket free verse, PublishAmerica, 2011. ISBN: 978-1142629787.
(6)   Good Kitty with ..., CreateSpace, 2013, ISBN: 978-149279333.

(7)   It's just a scratch, CreateSpace, 2013, ISBN: 978-1484156728.

(8)   Flowers and Sweets, CreateSpace, 2014, ISBN: 978-1495211843

(9)   Rock Hard Cupcake and Dead Fish, CreateSpace, 2013, ISBN: 978-1490433080.

(10)   Rock Hard Cupcake and Dead Fish, black and white version, CreateSpace, 2013, ISBN: 978-149792039.

(11)   Tainted Visions, CreateSpace, 2013, ISBN: 978-1495272189.

(12)   Visual Dissection, CreateSpace, 2013, ISBN: 978-1482797015.

(13)   Whatever Book, CreateSpace, 2013, ISBN: 978-149790653.

(14)   Zombie Stick Man Blues, CreateSpace, 2013, ISBN: 978-1483961200.

(15)   Where it comes from, CreateSpace, 2013, ISBN: 978-1484098868.

(16)   Mayan Free Verse, CreateSpace, 2014, ISBN: 978-1494912543.

(17)   OSM: WL Condition, CreateSpace, 2013, ISBN: 978-14848192870.

(18)   Scratching for a reason to live, CreateSpace, 2013, ISBN: 978-1484875988.

(19)   no captions needed: toy paintings/drawings, CreateSpace, 2013, ISBN: 978-1484940204.

(20)   Wayang Kulit : a painter's interpretation, CreateSpace, 2013, ISBN: 978-1490320083.

(21)   1, 2, 3 kitties : a cat counting book, PublishAmerica, 2008, ISBN: 978-160610848.

(22)   48708, +/-, &/or : an artist's life, CreateSpace, 2014, ISBN: 978-1494854232.

(23)   Gyotabstract, CreateSpace, 2014, ISBN: 978-1497361249.

IMAGES IN COLOR

Figure 35- NEXT PAGE- this image is of Saint Stanislaus Kostka
Church as explained in figure 24 but this time the building is
painted with acrylic paint. The manner of which I painted this
building is "expressive" reminiscent of the creative canvasses
of sides of beef done by my favorite painter, Chaim Soutine. Just
like the Soutine , my image using the warm colors like red in
the central part of Saint Stans Church is similar to the manner
of which Soutine painted the side of beef in warm colors. What
do you think ?

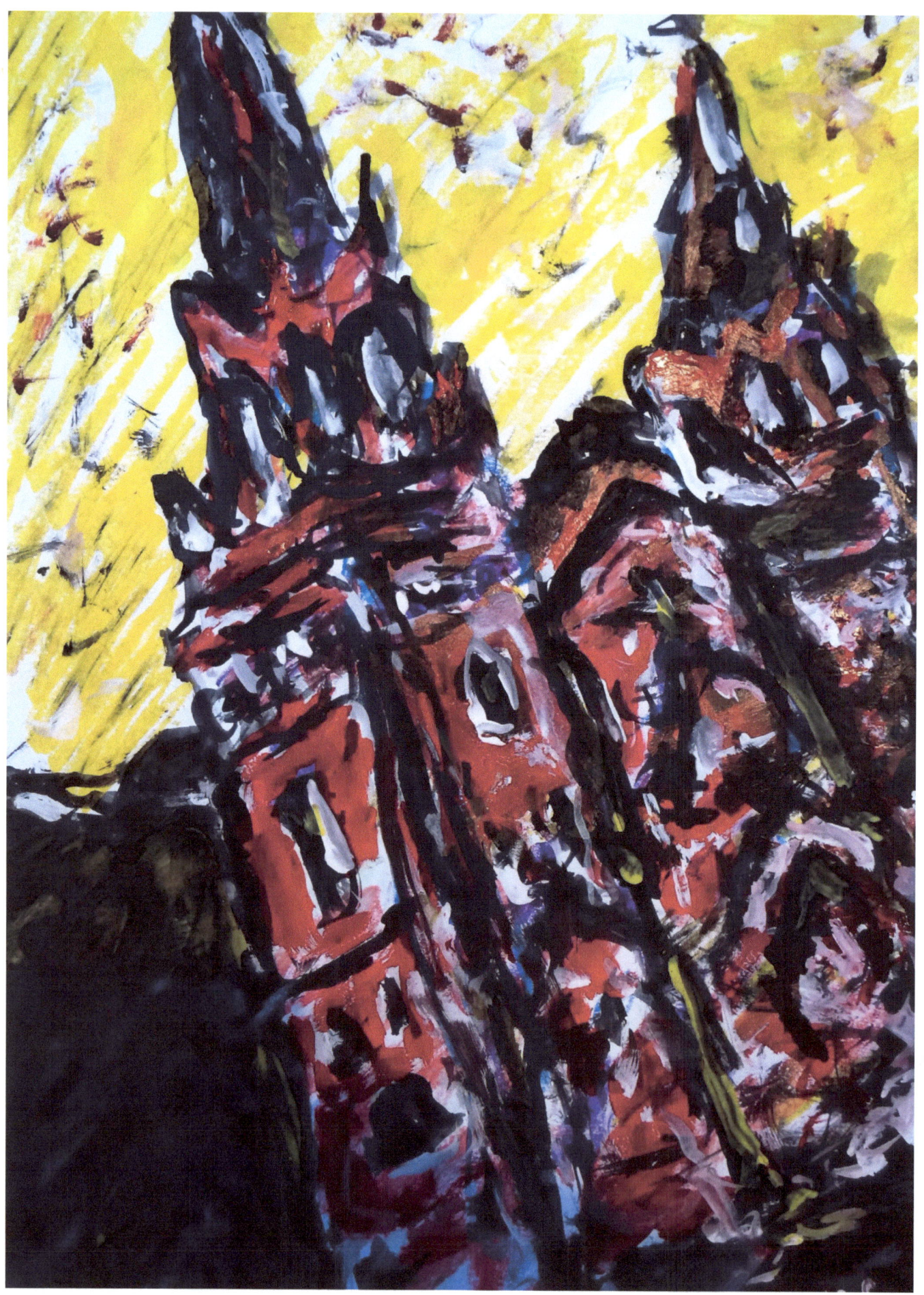

Figure 36- NEXT PAGE: this image is another image of the Bay County building as located at 515 Center Avenue. I contrast to figure 10 , this one uses acrylic paint to complete the image. THIS IS A SUCCESSFUL IMAGE !! WHAT DO YOU THINK ?

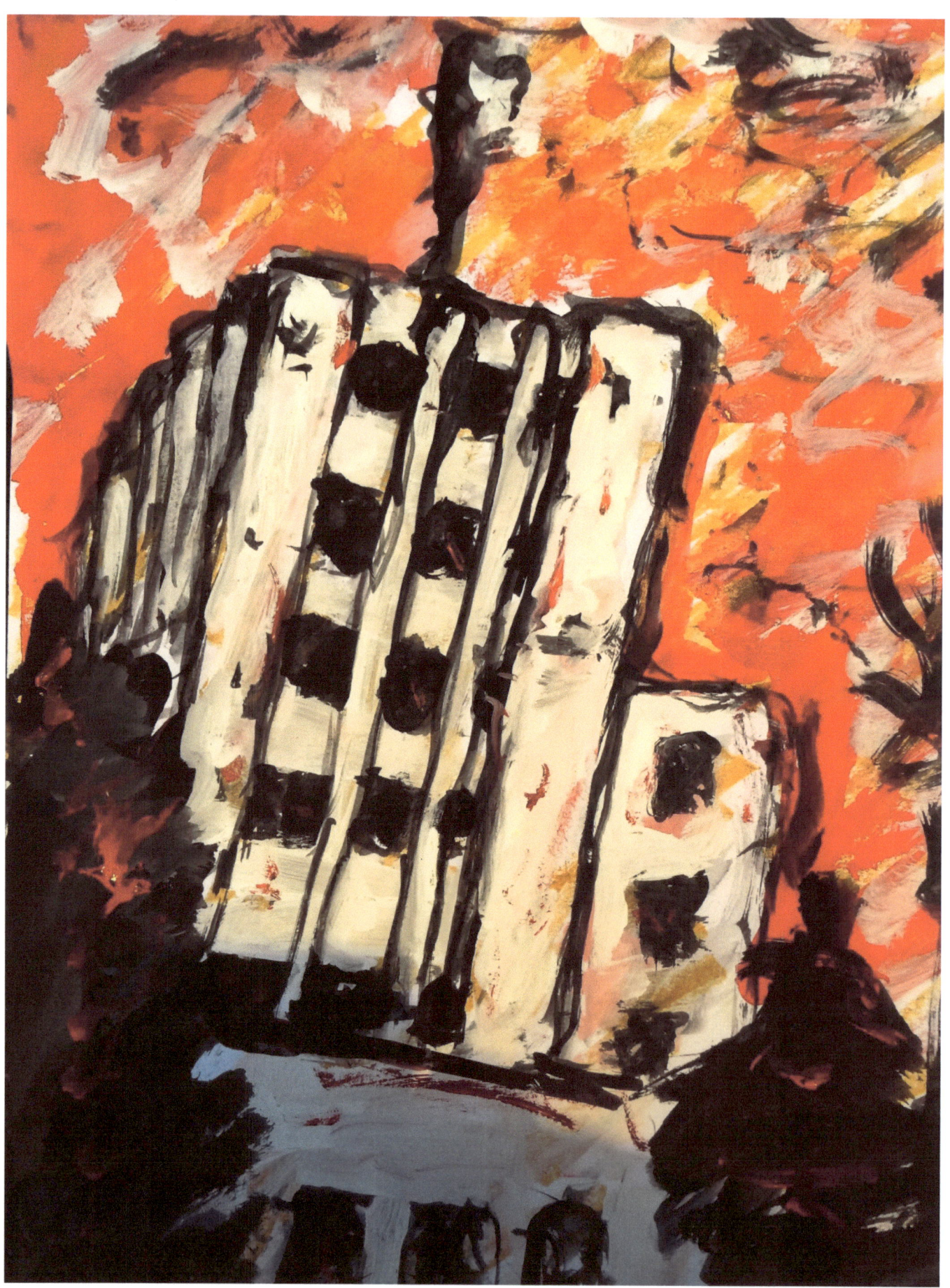

COMICS PREVIEW

The next couple of images are from an original comic I created called Rock Hard Cupcake. These pages are my first attempt at visual storytelling. I have had many positive reviews from these two pages telling the story of Rock Hard Cupcake losing a tooth.

What do you think?

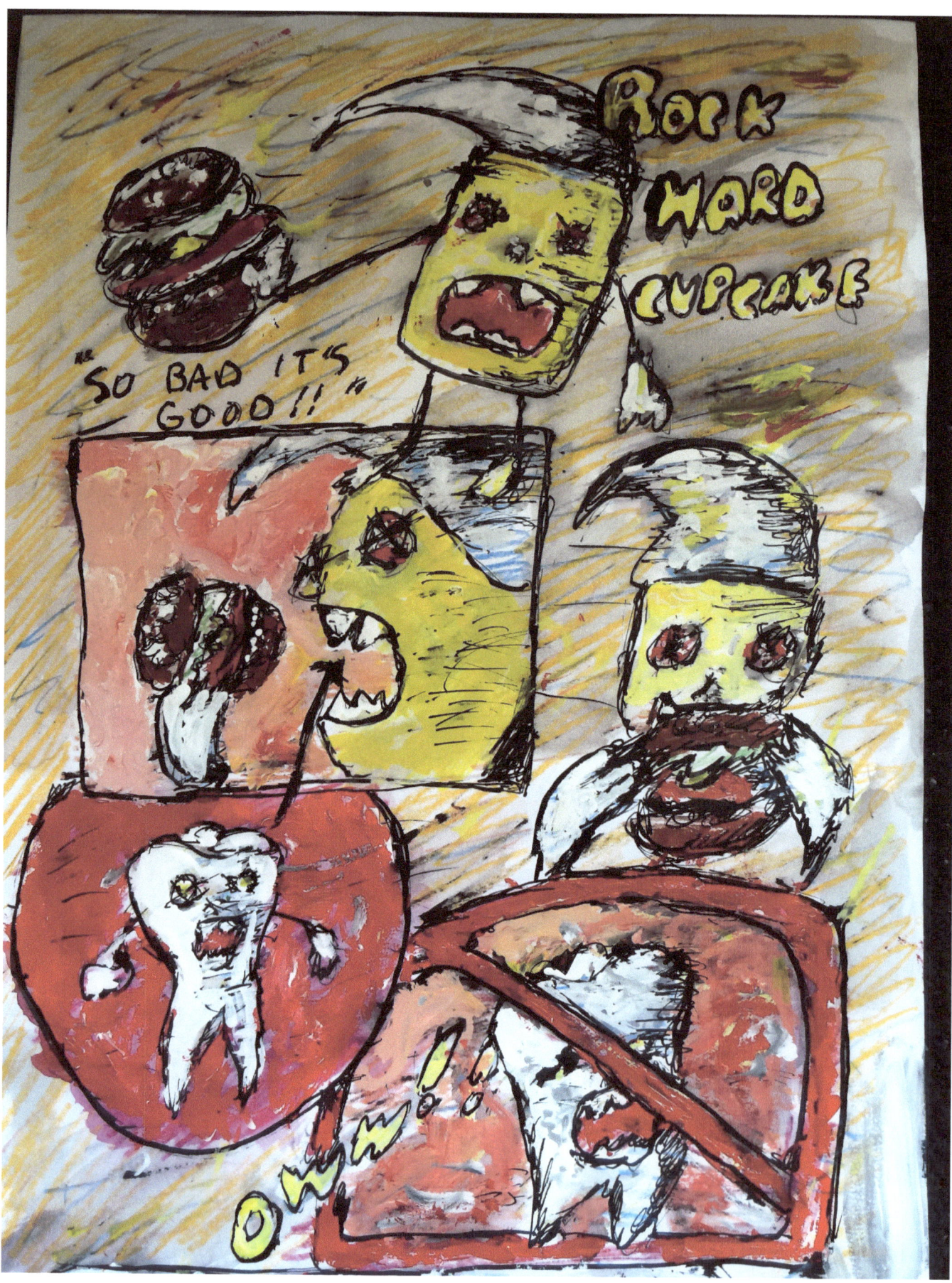

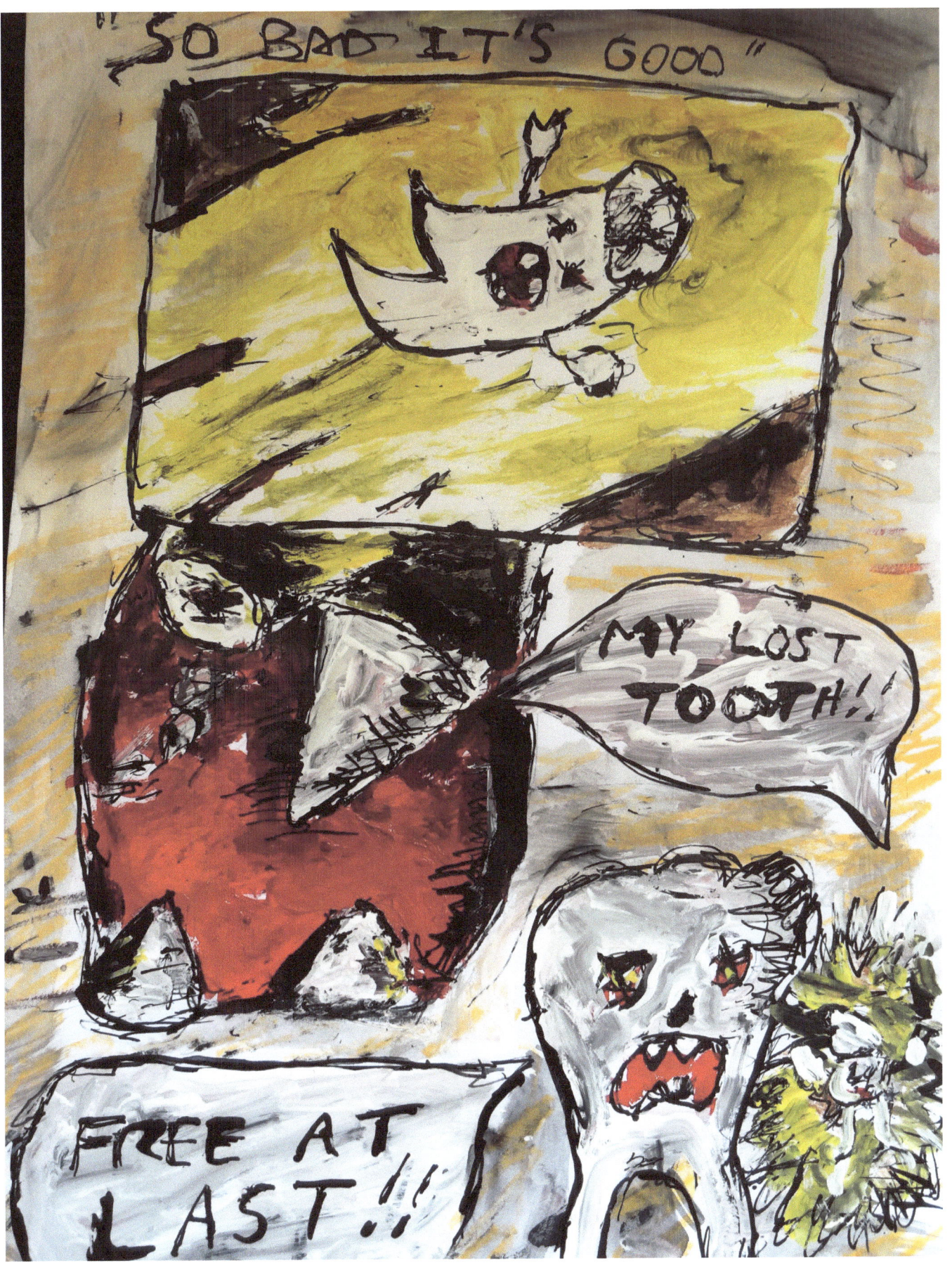

BE SURE TO CHECK OUT MY ORIGINAL COMIC

ROCK HARD CUPCAKE

THIS BOOK IS DEDICATED TO MY SON, CAMERON !!

Thanks for buying this book so that I can create another one!!!